WINNING THE INSIDE GAME

THE HANDBOOK OF ADVOCACY STRATEGIES

Foreword by Senator Jamie Raskin

ILIR ZHERKA

ISBN: 0615600611
ISBN 13: 9780615600611

TABLE OF CONTENTS

For Nej, Sef, and Medi.
Thank you for your love and support. I miss you.

To Linda, Alek, and Hana. You are my world.

ACKNOWLEDGMENTS[1]

As with advocacy campaigns, I needed a "coalition" of people to write this book.

First, I want to thank the many advocates who kindly gave their time and shared their experiences. Thanks to Johnny Barnes, Gary Bass, Sarah Dufendach, Wade Henderson, Josh Horwitz, Tanya Clay House, Rob Kampia, Meredith McGehee, Ralph Neas, Noah Winer, and Nancy Zirkin. Thanks also to the many Hill staffers, some who agreed to speak frankly, if anonymously, on topics of interest addressed in this book. Terry Lierman, Deborah Parkinson, and Ron Weich, who collectively have decades of experience working inside the hallowed halls of Congress, offered incredibly valuable insights.

My thanks go to Dr. Glenda Eoyang, who founded the field of Human Systems Dynamics. She is brilliant. The theories and tools she has developed with her sister Royce Holloday and others will be very useful to public interest advocates. I also want to thank Kristine Quade, Mary Nations, and Royce for introducing me to HSD during a very stimulating retreat in Minnesota and to Jeff Schwartz for helping me find them.

Many people helped me revise and edit the book. Thanks to Kathy Kretman, Abby Levine, Jennifer Matson, Mary Nations, Larry Ottinger, Karen Paul Stern, and Eli Zigas. I thank my research assistant, Diana Kelley Alvord. She conducted research, interviewed many of the advocates, and helped edit along the way. Special thanks to my wife, Linda Kinney, who served as an early editor, and to Senator Jamie Raskin for his powerful Foreword. Senator Raskin inspired a group of DC residents to found DC Vote in 1998 through his passionate description of a legal strategy that eventually became the *Alexander v. Daley* lawsuit.

---

1 Portions of this book rely on primary source information collected in a series of interviews with prominent advocates and Capitol Hill staffers, who decided to remain anonymous, between March 2009 and July 2010.

I want to also thank the Eugene and Agnes E. Meyer Foundation. This book is a direct result of the Exponent Award I received from the foundation. That award provided me with the initial resources and the encouragement to write this book. A subsequent grant by Meyer and Daniel Solomon allowed me to dive deeper into HSD. Thanks to Daniel for his support and for hiring me to serve as the Executive Director of DC Vote. Daniel gave me the opportunity of a lifetime.

FOREWARD BY SENATOR JAMIE RASKIN[2]

I had a professor in college, the political theorist Michael Walzer, who used to say that, "Politics is the art of doing the same thing over and over until one day it works."

That adage seems right to me but, of course, some movements and groups do the same thing over and over and it never works.

So anybody who cares about political results—especially people who believe that, at the deepest level, politics involves an important clash between justice and power—should study not just the art of doing politics, but the art of winning in politics. This excellent handbook is about how to win in the legislative arena. It is not about winning on the low road by buying politicians, corrupting officials, or destroying people's faith in government.

It is about winning by mastering the finest arts of democratic action—coalition-building, effective communication, popular mobilization, shrewd compromising—that keeps your principles intact.

Therefore, this manual is for anyone who wants to engage in serious-change politics and prevail, not just to sing really beautiful Joan Baez songs about what a glorious battle we lost when it is all over.

Yet, as hard-headed and practically focused as it is, this manual has a big heart. The author, Ilir Zherka, a natural-born organizer and political strategist who has been leading the fight for voting rights for the hundreds of thousands of Americans disenfranchised in the District of Columbia, knows that politics can uplift and transform people or it can denigrate and trample them. So his creative methodology links positive purposes in the public interest with effective techniques that constantly move the cause of social progress and public dignity forward. Like the great, pragmatic popular organizers and legislative strategists

---

2 Maryland State Senator and Professor of Constitutional Law at American University.

of our history—people like Bayard Rustin, Bob Moses, Joe Rauh, Ralph Neas, Paul Wellstone, Dorothy Height, and Wade Henderson—Ilir knows in his heart the integral connection between means and ends.

Of course, ever since Machiavelli cast his spell on the princes of the world, many people who fashion themselves political "realists" and "insiders" have argued that politics is essentially corrupt and that political success requires, above all, a willingness to do outrageous and immoral things. They contend that all political means are equally suited to all political ends.

But people who have championed the cause of democracy and equal rights, like the movement for voting rights for people who live in the nation's capital, know that certain political means go with the side of power and corruption while other means go with movements for change and democratic reform.

This book is for people who want to work in politics, not for narrow, special interests, but to make things better and fairer for everyone. Still, it's sharp enough, it's insightful enough, it's readable enough, it's quotable enough, and it's so surpassingly useful, that I am afraid it might find an audience among the adversaries of change too.

This is a disturbing thought. So, please, my friends, read this soon-to-be indispensable guide for public-interest legislative organizers; study it and analyze it; give it to your close friends and colleagues; use it to change the world we live in.

But, whatever you do, please don't tell anybody about it who you wouldn't want making public policy for you and your family.

We can't afford to see it fall into the wrong hands.

—JBR, May 22, 2011

INTRODUCTION

It was the fall of 1993, and my job search had taken me to Washington, DC. I had just returned from a year working in Albania to assist with the transition to democracy there. After a day of exhausting informational interviews on Capitol Hill, unsure of my next career steps, I discovered the Trover Shop, a landmark bookstore on the Hill[1]. Naturally, I was perusing the political section when I came across a short book with a snappy title – *Hardball*. It was written by Chris Matthews, a former staffer for Speaker Tip O'Neill and current MSNBC host of a news show with the same name. I skimmed the book right in the shop. Matthews did a great job sharing some of the lessons he learned on the Hill — things like the importance of loyalty, the need to respond to all negative attacks, and the utility of turning someone's perceived strength into a weakness. I especially appreciated the way Matthews used stories to illustrate his lessons.

I bought *Hardball* and it became a bible of sorts for me over the next several years as I navigated the political arena in DC. I found myself referring back to it over and over again through my jobs as legislative counsel for Congressman George Miller, as ethnic outreach director for the Clinton-Gore reelection campaign, and ultimately as the executive director of the advocacy organization DC Vote.

Not long after I began my job at DC Vote in 2002, I had the privilege of organizing a group of high-powered non-profit leaders on a transformative panel called "Lessons Learned from the Coalition Battlefield." Sponsored by the Business School Career Center of George Washington University and organized by DC Vote and Common Cause, the panel brought together leaders of several large-scale coalition efforts from the recent past to exchange lessons they had learned from fighting their civil rights issues on the political front, in coalition groups.

XI

What I took away from that day I spent on the "Lessons Learned" panel has stayed with me throughout the eight years that I, along with DC Vote's board, staff, and thousands of grassroots supporters, have been battling to bring legislative voting representation to the residents of the District of Columbia.

Given the long-lasting resonance of that panel discussion, for several years now I have been thinking that I needed to write my own handbook for those, like me, who have dedicated themselves to changing the world through advocacy. And here it is. Whether you are in your first public interest job, learning the political ropes on Capitol Hill, or you are a seasoned organizational leader and advocate, this book was written for you.

I have brought together the best practices and wisdom on advocacy, and combined them into ten top advocacy strategies, told through the stories I have lived and the experiences of some of the top advocates in the country. Since I am a visual learner, I have included a few important diagrams that may help you internalize the lessons I have learned. To illustrate some of the strategies, my research assistant, Diana Kelly Alvord, and I interviewed some leading advocates in Washington, DC, as well as senior legislative staffers. I included their stories in each of the chapters to provide additional examples of each principle.

Another wonderful opportunity I have had during my tenure at DC Vote was attending training sessions in Minnesota and Washington, DC designed to provide tools for understanding and shaping group dynamics. The model introduced to me at this training, Human Systems Dynamics (HSD), is a collection of theory and tools that help make sense of the patterns that emerge when people interact in groups, families, organizations, and communities.[2] HSD struck me as an excellent behavioral science and analytic tool that can help advocates better understand Congress and the way things work inside its hallowed halls. As such, I have adapted some of the more easy-to-understand tools for the purposes of these top ten advocacy strategies. I believe that this is an innovative way to approach advocacy work. I hope that introducing this model will add tremendous value to the field of advocacy. Executive directors and the in-house lobbyists at non-profit organizations will find these tools especially useful for understanding and influencing the patterns around them.

Although my point of reference is the U.S. Congress, these principles and tools are applicable to any advocacy campaign targeting any group of policy-makers. Whether you are in Sacramento, California; Albany, New York; or Prishtina, Kosova, as long you are advocating for a new law, this book is for you.

Perhaps like you, I appreciate brevity. Therefore, I have purposely kept this book short. In fact, for those who want to get right to the strategies, I have provided a summary in the following section and a full list in the appendix. For ease of use, I have divided each chapter in the book into four sections – The Story, Additional Stories, The Tools, and The Bottom Line.

This book is designed to be a reference tool, to be read and used over and over again. Its tenets are simple and straightforward; it provides a road map to successful advocacy in an arcane, complex, and very diverse universe full of legislative and executive bodies throughout America and abroad. I hope that you can take my experiences and the advice of others in this book and spin them into your own advocacy victory, and that this short book will serve you well in your mission. Remember, no one story provides all the answers for how to best apply the principles in this book. And no two stories are exactly alike. Your advocacy campaign will be entirely unique, and you'll create it with entirely new patterns of behavior.

Becoming a good advocate, as Nancy Zirkin, executive vice president of the Leadership Conference on Civil and Human Rights, puts it, "takes years and you learn as you go." My goal is to give you a significant leg up by sharing the strategies that she, I, and so many other advocates have learned over many, many years and many, many battles. Enjoy.

Brief History of DC Voting Rights

I draw extensively from my experiences in the fight to secure DC voting rights. So that you understand the context of the examples I provide in this book, here's a brief history of the DC Democracy Movement.

An angry mob of Revolutionary War veterans assembled outside the building in Philadelphia where Congress had convened in 1783. The veterans were unruly and threatening. The delegates called on the governor and legislature of Pennsylvania to protect the Congress. They refused. The Congress fled, and this experience later informed the Constitutional Convention's decision to carve out a special territory over which Congress would have exclusive authority.[3] They did not decide, however, any of the other major questions regarding that territory: where it would be located; the form of local government; the relationship between the local government and the federal government; and what form of representation the people in the capital would have in the U.S. Congress itself. None of these things are spelled out in the Constitution.

This was Congress' "Original Punt." There was no consensus position on any of these questions. There was, however, a general assumption that the capital would likely be located within an existing state such as Philadelphia or New York, the two largest cities that had hosted the federal government. But, the South pushed for a more neutral location. The North and South agreed to a compromise: the capital would be located in territory taken from both Virginia and Maryland. The two states offered land for the federal capital which Congress accepted in 1790 with the understanding that local laws would remain in effect until that the federal government assumed jurisdiction over the area in 1800. During this ten year period, the people who lived in the capital before it was fully constituted continued to vote in their respective states for members of Congress.

In 1801, Congress punted again. The "states' rights" Democratic-Republicans defeated the Federalists, who supported a strong central government, in the election of 1800. Before the Democratic-Republicans could take over the Congress and the White House, the Federalists pushed through "The Organic Act," which fully constituted the District of Columbia and eliminated representation in Congress. Again, it did not deal with any of the other major questions.

There was a strong outcry locally against the Act. The DC democracy movement was born that year, as people fought against taxation without representation.[4] But, because DC residents were so few in number and the challenges facing the young nation were so great, they made very little traction. For most of the next century and a half, the residents of what became Washington, DC, could not vote for president, had limited or no locally-elected government, and did not enjoy any voting representation in Congress.

The Movement started to win victories during the civil rights era of the 20th Century. DC residents won the right to vote for president in 1961 with the passage of the 23rd amendment. In the early 1970s, DC won "home rule," which included the right to elect a local mayor, council, and delegate to the Congress. Congress, however, reserved the right to veto and rewrite DC's local laws, including the budget. DC's delegate to the Congress would be treated like those from the territories: she would not have voting power. These limitations led some folks in DC to refer to this status as "Home Fool."

Beginning in the late 1970s, people in DC mobilized around two divergent approaches to securing full democracy. One campaign was based on the desire to secure voting representation in Congress without changing DC's character as the national capital. The other campaign focused on turning the District into the 51st state called New Columbia.

In 1978, Congress passed the DC Voting Rights Amendment to the Constitution. It was ratified by only sixteen of the thirty-eight states necessary for it to be adopted. In 1993, Congress considered and rejected a DC statehood bill, by a vote of 153 to 277. In 2000, the Supreme Court let stand a lower court ruling in *Alexander v. Daley* that DC residents were not entitled as citizens under the Constitution to representation in Congress. The Court suggested that an act of Congress would be necessary to provide representation.

DC Vote was founded in 1998 to support this court challenge and to pursue an advocacy campaign for full representation in Congress. In 2009, DC Vote also publicly embraced DC statehood as its ultimate objective.

Summarizing the Strategies

Advocates typically view advocacy as an effort to work both the "outside game" by engaging grassroots supporters and the "inside game" by lobbying legislators and their staff directly.[5]

Organizations engaged in advocacy spend considerable resources on the outside game – recruiting grassroots supporters; deciding on priorities; activating those supporters; and generating news stories. On top of those goals, most such organizations also: issue reports; update their websites; host events; send fundraising appeals; write grant proposals; and hire, train, and manage employees. All of those activities are important. You need to engage and empower the people that are affected by the problem you're trying to solve; otherwise your cause and your organization will lack the legitimacy and power necessary to win. It would also lack the energy and the funds needed to get things accomplished. But, these outside game strategies, and the administrative work that supports them, are designed ultimately to win the inside game.

The inside game revolves around people in the legislative and executive branches of government. These folks hold significant decision-making power. They decide whether to hold hearings on your issue, introduce a bill, and pass it. Once it becomes law, they also decide how they will implement that law. While policymakers are susceptible to grassroots pressure, an advocate must learn how to combine the outside and inside games to win. Here are the ten principles that will help you do just that.

I Frame Your Issue First

First, frame your request for legislative change in a way that maximizes legislative support. Gauge the reaction of the legislature and their staff before you decide what you ask for and how you talk about it. Conduct polls and focus groups, where possible, as you are developing your message.

II Recruit the Right Legislative Champions

All legislative efforts are dependent on legislative "champions" taking up your cause and doing the hard work to get a bill passed through a legislative body. Find the right champion by figuring out which legislative committee has jurisdiction over your issue. Try to attract the legislator who is both passionate about your issue and has power (i.e., the person who has seniority and perhaps is chair or ranking member). When you find your champion(s), remember that his or staff plays a pivotal role in how effective you will be. Cultivate a relationship of trust with the staff and stay in frequent contact.

III Secure Votes by Avoiding Extremes

At the federal level, you need sixty votes in the US Senate, a majority of the House, and the signature of the President to get your legislation enacted into law. At the local and state level, you need a majority and sometimes a super majority to advance your goals. Where possible, begin the legislative process by recruiting bipartisan and/or broad support at the outset. To get bipartisan support, develop a bill that will attract a range of legislative champions, and, thereby, significantly increase your chances of success.

IV Join or Create a Working Coalition

Coalitions are needed to popularize an issue, capture the attention of the media, and attract champions. Just as important — they are necessary to help with generating grassroots support, lobbying legislators, and working the executive branch. At the federal level, coalitions help you target specific districts in the states by asking people to contact their members of Congress. Expect different levels of commitment and engagement from different coalition members. Coalitions require on going efforts and hard work to keep the movement alive, even when there is little or no legislative action. One tactic to employ to keep momentum and enthusiasm high is to work toward specified milestones and interim "wins."

V Empower the Grassroots

The people who are most directly affected by the problem you are trying to solve are among your strongest advocates — give them a voice. Ask people to perform specific tasks like contacting legislators or attending a rally. Give people the opportunity to be creative in their advocacy — they may surprise you and give your movement some real momentum.

VI Use the Outside Game to Influence Policymakers

Winning the inside game starts with recruiting outside supporters. Engage in activities outside the halls of Congress, the state house, or city hall that generate news stories because they impact perceptions among the inside players. Create a cycle where outside activities result in media stories, which result in more legislative attention, which feeds your recruitment of people for grassroots activities. Ultimately, most of your activities should be used to increase your presence and influence in the legislature.

VII Communicate at All Times in All Directions

Organizations have to communicate at all times in all directions. You cannot assume that your message is getting through to the right people or that they understand it. The most effective way to communicate with people is by talking to them directly. Utilize all the modern tools of communication, but concentrate on direct engagement with people. Also, create and maintain a well-organized, comprehensive website.

VIII Work the Inside Game

Place a premium on direct interaction with legislators and their staff. Ensure you can provide quality information on a moment's notice. Be honest and straightforward with your legislative allies. Seek access to legislators by attending fundraisers and/or other events whenever possible. Follow through on your commitments and follow up to ensure legislators and their staffs are doing what they promised. Although the inside game matters a great deal, you have to master the other strategies in this book before you even get in the game.

IX Elections Matter

Remember that elections matter. One senior legislative staffer put it succinctly: "Politicians are all about getting re-elected." Therefore, the most effective way to get a member of Congress or other legislator to help you is to demonstrate how, by supporting you, they can get reelected. Or, show how opposing you will threaten their reelection. The strongest advocacy organizations in the country understand this principle. They produce scorecards rating legislators' votes and disseminate them widely. They give campaign contributions and sponsor advertisements. And, most importantly, they motivate people to vote for or against a candidate, ultimately affecting election prospects. Remember: for the elected officials you're hoping to influence, it's all about getting reelected.

X You Lose Until You Win

Advocacy fights are usually marathons, not sprints. Public policy changes are won through movements, and movements must be sustained over a period time with regular activities designed to keep stakeholders engaged and enthusiastic about the goal. Be persistent, determined, and optimistic about your chances of success over the long haul. You will "lose" many times before you win. Additionally, getting a bill enacted into law is just the first step. You have to work then to ensure that the executive branch is implementing the law correctly and that it is serving its original purpose.

Introducing Human Systems Dynamic

There is a saying in Washington that you can get a lot done if you don't care who gets the credit. Staffers, lobbyists, and advocates are fond of repeating this line. After all, we do a lot of work without receiving full recognition. But there's a greater truth at work here: the legislative process is a very complex system. From committees to elected officials to legislative leaders to government agencies and the White House, an enormous number of people are involved in enacting a bill into law (all of which is true at the state and local level, as well). Add in advocates and lobbyists, and it is easy to see how the system is totally interdependent and unpredictable. Human systems dynamic theorists call such a system "dynamical" (a term taken from the natural sciences to describe complex systems). A system is dynamical when events are emerging from multiple influences over time and where changes are often the result of multiple causes. This system conjures up another oft-repeated DC line: "There are two things you never want to see made — sausages and laws."

So, how do you navigate through this labyrinth and turn your idea into the law of the land? A great place to start is by understanding some basic truths: people in all human systems develop patterns of behavior; while the results are unpredictable, we can use tools to figure out what patterns are in play and how to influence those patterns.

Under HSD, there are simple rules that govern complex systems. Some people describe these rules as a "culture." Essentially, these rules govern how people in the system will behave, how decisions will be made, and what issues rise to the top:

> "Simple rules establish patterns, interaction, and decision-making that govern individual and group behavior... Simple rules are generally unspoken and they influence the organization in ways that are not recognized by its members."[6]

In this book, you will discover techniques that will help guide your strategic decisions — how you frame your issue, find legislative champions, and use grassroots supporters — so that you can win the inside game. Simple rules govern your overall approach and behavior. They exist, whether or not you articulate them. Because we are being mindful about our strategies and our approach, here's my list for the five simple rules that are present for most successful advocates.

SIMPLE RULES FOR ADVOCATES

- Commit to a long-term struggle
- Be adaptive about your position and strategy

- Be honest with your legislative champions and their staff
- Interact with your stakeholders directly and often
- Unite people and other organizations around your mission

The U.S. Congress and other legislative bodies operate through simple rules as well. Here's a list of the top five I put together with the help of some experienced lobbyists, advocates, and legislative staffers.

SIMPLE RULES FOR LEGISLATORS

- Cater to the needs of your constituents first
- Make and keep relationships with other legislators
- Work across the aisle to get things done
- Get leadership and committee chair support for your bills
- Recognize the central role of your staff

Of course, we could come up with many other rules that apply to advocates and legislators. But, for simple rules to work, the list must be short enough for you to memorize and recall them, and universal enough for them to have meaning over space and time.

I recognize that we could add another simple rule for legislators in this age of hyper-partisanship. Perhaps something like "never give in to your opponents," or "no law is better than supporting a compromise." Even in times where politics are polarized, it is still true that legislators must work across the aisle in most legislatures, especially the US Congress, to pass bills that get signed into law.

Throughout this book, you will find tools to evaluate your strategies and adapt more effectively. Here's the first tool, the landscape diagram[7]:

Diagram 1: The Landscape Diagram

The landscape diagram provides an excellent tool for considering the patterns at work in an advocacy campaign. On any given day, problems emerge or become clear to people. People then share opinions and ideas with each other or make demands on their elected officials. These are occurring in the Unorganized Zone. Inside Congress, there are a host of activities also in that zone — letters, press releases, media interviews, etc., — around bills that have very little support. These ideas are in that zone because there is very little agreement about whether they should become law, and very little certainty about whether or not a bill will even be considered.

In the 110th Congress (2006-2008), nearly 14,000 bills were introduced and yet, in total, only 449 of those bills were enacted during that entire session of Congress.[8] The 110th was typical of most modern Congresses. My goal is to help you move your idea through the legislative process by creating the impetus for hearings, studies, and bill introductions as you and your legislative champions move into in the Self-Organizing Zone. Of course, your primary objective is to create broad agreement among key players in Congress and the certainty that your idea should receive priority treatment by a legislative committee and on the floor of the House and Senate. For it is here, in the Organized Zone, where you will win the inside game and make your idea the law of the land.

I. Frame Your Issue First

Your message and legislative strategy are deeply intertwined and must be developed through research.

The Story

It was November 1993. Opponents of statehood for Washington, DC defeated the New Columbia Admission Act by a vote of 153 to 277. The act would have turned the District of Columbia into the fifty-first state by shrinking the capital to the National Mall and the federal buildings, and allowing the nearly 600,000 people who lived in DC to form a state. Of those opposed, 172 were Republicans and 105 were Democrats.[9] Proponents asked, rightly, how could this happen? Bill Clinton had won the presidency, and Democrats controlled both chambers of Congress. In fact, Democrats had backed statehood for a decade. They were now in power. Many in DC believed the time had come for the birth of New Columbia.

The DC statehood movement, however, framed the issue in a way that does not immediately appeal to a majority of people and demands a lot of explanations. I strongly support DC statehood. But, many House Democrats were opposed to making DC the fifty-first state, including some leading Democrats from the DC area such as Representatives Steny Hoyer and Jim Moran.[10] Their resistance reflected popular opinion.[11] Why? Because the "statehood" message gets people asking the wrong questions: isn't DC too small to become a state? Didn't the Founding Fathers intentionally disenfranchise DC residents? Where would we put the fifty-first star on the US flag? Of course, DC has more people living in it than Wyoming and almost as many as seven other states. Additionally, there is no evidence that the Founders intended to disenfranchise DC residents. And, hey, the flag looks really cool with fifty-one stars! That discussion, however, diverts attention from the very strong, and immediately understood argument that tax-paying Americans living in our nation's capital deserve full citizenship with equal rights to representation in Congress and local control over local affairs.[12]

Local lawyer and philanthropist Daniel Solomon and his close friend, city planner Joe Sternlieb, understood this when they met around Daniel's kitchen table in 1997, four years after the disheartening defeat of the DC Statehood Bill. They realized that if they and the other residents of the District of Columbia were ever to have a voice in Congress, a fundamental right of every American living outside DC, *both* the message, as well as the legislative objective, had to change. While this chapter focuses on framing the issues, that change is not enough. You must implement all the strategies together to be successful.

Daniel and Joe decided to create an organization, the Coalition for DC Representation in Congress Education Fund (smartly renamed "DC Vote" a year later), with a mission to secure only voting representation in Congress and not statehood. Their message: the treatment of Washingtonians amounted to taxation without representation. With that battle cry, they launched an ambitious effort to remake and recharge a movement that had been defeated and worn-down.

Fast-forward to 2006: DC Vote conducted focus groups in Ohio, state polls in Ohio and Texas, and a national poll. We confirmed that Daniel and Joe's original focus on representation was right on. We learned that strong majorities— 82 percent in 2005 and 2009 polls— believed that representation in Congress was an American birthright.[13] Likewise, the responders and interviewees reacted most positively to the idea that people who paid taxes should have representation in Congress. After all, we fought a revolution in 1776 to end taxation without representation!

In 2007, 242 members of the US House of Representatives and fifty-seven senators voted for the DC Voting Rights Act. Here's what one of our strongest opponents had to say about the issue:

Mr. PRICE of Georgia. Mr. Speaker, I thank my colleague [Tom Davis] from Virginia for his leadership on this and for yielding. I want to stipulate at the beginning of this statement that I support enfranchisement, strongly support enfranchisement for the citizens of the District of Columbia. However, the oath that I take on the first day of our session stipulates that I uphold and defend the Constitution of the United States, and I believe firmly that the Constitution will not allow this. . .[14]

Clearly, by reframing the debate, we won the rhetorical fight on this bill. Even our opponents expressed support for the idea of DC voting representation in Congress. In the past, these folks felt very comfortable opposing statehood outright. More importantly, we dramatically increased the number of votes we received for the DC Voting Rights Act, a bill based on the idea of representation and not on creating the fifty-first state. It is worth noting here that DC Vote publicly embraced statehood in 2009 as our ultimate objective. But we talk about achieving full equality and democracy because "statehood" can be confusing for lots of people outside DC. While the general public and many members of Congress oppose the concept of DC statehood, activists in DC and members of the DC Council view statehood as synonymous with full equality and democracy. That message, repeated over and over for decades, became sacrosanct for many. But this is the danger of getting the framing wrong at the outset because folks do become as emotionally attached to their message as people are to their national flags. Even though statehood is the objective of the DC democracy movement, it must be framed as a fight for equality and democracy because Americans support those rights. By framing your issue correctly, people in and outside of Congress are much more open to hearing your arguments and potentially supporting your cause.

Additional Stories[15]

The debate over recognizing same-sex marriage in the District of Columbia provides an instructive example of the important role of message framing. As part of their strategy to legalize gay marriage in 2009, advocates changed from framing the issue as "gay marriage" to "marriage equality," based on polling data. One gay rights advocate emphasized the importance of framing the message in terms of equality, civil rights, and family rights. He said: "You don't want to turn people off before they hear what you are talking about."[16]

The climate change issue is another example of the importance of framing your issue correctly at the outset. President Barack Obama made climate change legislation one of his major goals in 2009. The Congress responded. The House passed a major cap-and-trade bill in the summer of 2009. The effort in the Senate proceeded much more slowly, but steadily toward a compromise bill. With the loss of the Democrats' sixty-seat (filibuster proof) majority in January 2010 (Scott Brown, a Republican, was elected to replace Ted Kennedy after his death), the climate bill was already in doubt. But a force of nature and a lingering framing issue seemed to change the legislative dynamics considerably. A massive snow storm hit the DC area in early February, dumping over three feet in a seven-day period, breaking a one-hundred-year record. The federal government was closed for four days and the House and Senate were closed as well during that week.

Republicans and their allies pounced. Knowing that environmentalists and scientists had framed the issue early on as "global warming," they pointed to the snowstorm as evidence that global warming didn't exist.[17] Proponents of legislation had realized a few years ago that they made a serious framing mistake and switched to "climate change." But, by mid-February of 2010, Democrats and Republicans alike were predicting the death of the cap-and-trade legislation because, among other things, the snowstorm made it more difficult to prove that global warming is a real phenomenon![18]

Environmentalists like Al Gore seemed to understand that they had a serious framing problem. To thwart the attacks from the right, they launched ads during the 2010 storm that talked about securing jobs from clean energy. The ads said nothing about climate science.[19]

Clearly, framing your issue properly is not always easy. Oftentimes, advocates use language that intuitively feels "right" to them, or that resonates with their supporters. "Statehood" is a term that resonates strongly and emotionally with a great many people in DC. It is what we want and demand because it would make DC residents equal citizens. "Gay marriage" is descriptive of the end result desired by gay rights advocates. And advocates may even have tested, through polls and focus groups, the term "global warming." In each of these cases, the initial framing did not work well enough with the general population and, therefore, needed to evolve. Recall Simple Rule number two for advocates: you must be open to changing the way you frame your issue to succeed.

The Tools: Understanding Containers, Differences, and Exchanges

While the best way to test framing is to commission polls and focus groups, doing so is very expensive. Most public-interest advocacy groups do not have the resources to do extensive research. Additionally, once you find a message and framing that resonates with average people, you still need to understand the patterns of behavior you will generate. HSD provided the below model to help you understand those patterns.

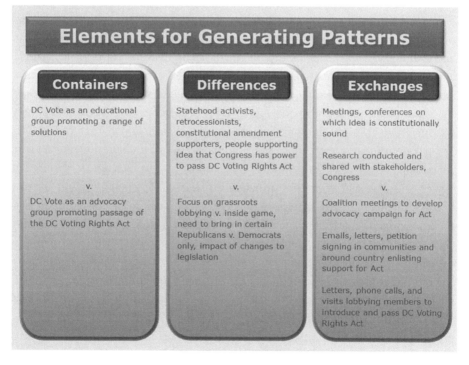

Diagram 2: The CDE Table

The CDE Table reflects the combination of context, differences, and communications that leads to *all* human patterns of behavior. C stands for containers, D is for differences, and E is for exchanges. Containers can be just about anything— the structure of your organization, your mission, your decision-making process, your message, your messenger, etc. The way to figure out your container is to ask: what binds us together? What is common among us?

Differences represent the range of perspectives, experiences, and beliefs that each person or group brings to a conversation or task. A good way to think about differences is to ask: among us together, what differences, experiences, and perspectives are represented? How are those differences manifested in relationship to the container?

Exchanges are the means through which people interact directly or indirectly. Think about different ways we engage within a coalition or organization and beyond (i.e., via e-mail and in meetings, through articles and protests, in organizations and individually, etc.).

Using Diagram 2, we would say that within the DC Voting Rights Coalition our container was the fight for voting representation in Congress. The differences within our coalition were represented by organizations that were formed around religion, good government, civil rights, social services, and political affiliation. These different missions lead to different perspectives. The exchanges within our coalition were accomplished via e-mail notices, regular meetings, phone calls, letters to Congress, issue memos, and the like.

All human interaction has a C, D, and E. The interplay of CDEs creates patterns of behavior.

Use Diagram 2 to figure out your container(s). Identifying your container will help you identify the differences that will be highlighted around that container. You can then decide if those are the differences that you want accentuated. If not, adjust your message and container. Most groups make subconscious decisions about which "container" they use to frame their issue. That is a mistake.

If you have the resources, conduct polling and focus groups to figure out your message. Even with this information, however, you will still need to interpret which specific message works for you. So, whether or not you have resources, use the Container, Differences, and Exchanges model to figure out how your organization and its supporters talk about what you do. Then ask yourself how your target populations— constituents, legislators, donors— will react to that message. Figure out what differences of opinion and debate your container will draw out. Then figure out if those are the differences you want people to focus on. If not, change your container.

Let's review the above diagram for an example of how different "containers" lead to different results. When DC Vote was solely focused on education, all the differences and exchanges were around the best options for change. When the container switched to an advocacy group pushing a specific piece of legislation, the differences and exchanges focused on the bill – is it the right bill, how do we get it through Congress, etc. By shifting our container (approach and focus), we dramatically changed both the way people responded to us and the work in which we engaged.

The Bottom Line

1. First, frame your request for change in a way that maximizes legislative and public support.

2. Conduct polls and focus groups, if possible, when developing your message.

3. Apply the Container, Differences, and Exchanges concept to figure out the best way to frame your issue.

4. Gauge the reaction of legislators and their staff before you decide what you ask for and how you talk about it.

II. Recruit the Right Champions

Your champions will be essential during the legislative process, so choose wisely and build a relationship of trust.

The Story

The good news traveled fast. In June 2003, a DC Vote supporter e-mailed me to say that Republican Congressman Tom Davis from Virginia had just declared on Mark Plotkin's WTOP radio program that he thought DC should get a seat in the House of Representatives by joining it with a seat for Utah. "Bingo!" I thought. Back in 2002, Congressman David Bonior from Michigan told me that the key to passing DC voting rights was to come up with something to give to potential opponents. He said, "You have to give your opponents something in exchange for their vote, and it can't just be that they will feel good about doing the right thing." In other words, create self-interest among your opponents and you will get a bipartisan bill. I remember thinking back then, "What can our allies in Congress give our opponents? A bridge? A post office? Some other earmark?" It seemed like the things legislators would normally "trade" would not be appropriate in the case of DC voting rights. Davis, however, offered an idea that would become the foundation of the bill that we would promote.

Perhaps, more importantly, we recognized that Tom Davis was a potential Republican champion at a time when Republicans controlled both chambers of Congress and the White House. Davis had just led a successful effort by the Republicans in 2002 to expand their seats in the House. He had lots of political capital with conservatives. Davis also represented a neighboring congressional district in Northern Virginia. Most importantly, he was the chairman of the House Governmental Reform Committee, the very committee that had jurisdiction over the District of Columbia. In short: Davis was the right legislative champion. We needed a champion to introduce legislation, organize hearings, attract outside help, push for markups, and get a vote on the floors of the House and Senate.

We set about the task of cultivating a relationship with him by first earning the trust of his staff. DC Vote was still viewed as a grassroots advocacy organization that was mostly working the outside game, and therefore unpredictable and unreliable because we didn't have Hill relationships. To soften our approach, we asked the League of Women Voters, a collegial organization with whom we had a strong relationship, to request the meeting. We brought along another one of our partners, the DC Appleseed Center for Law and Justice, to lend still more legitimacy. Appleseed had worked with Davis previously and was viewed as a credible and moderate organization.

Nonetheless, Jim Moore, Davis's staffer, viewed us warily. He was unsure if we were friend or foe. Our job was to make him comfortable with us, but also to get Davis to rethink his initial novel idea, which was to make DC part of Maryland for purposes of representation only. We were in a bind because we wanted to show respect for his creativity. We also knew that most Washingtonians did not want to be a part of Maryland. So, we offered to objectively review Davis' idea.

At the same time, we had to protect our relationship with our existing champion, DC Delegate Eleanor Holmes Norton. We supported Norton's introduction of the No Taxation Without Representation. Act earlier that year. The bill provided for two senators, in addition to a House member. It represented the full aspirations and expectations of DC residents in terms of voting representation in Congress. Norton suggested, and we agreed, that we would report to her the results of our "study," of Davis' Maryland idea, Latham & Watkins, a major law firm in DC that had provided pro bono legal counsel for many years, concluded that it would be unconstitutional for DC residents to vote for Maryland senators. We also concluded that the bill would be politically unviable. The District would likely be separated into two Maryland congressional districts, or merge into a part of Maryland, because the population of DC is not large enough to constitute a single congressional district.

Our goal was to report this bad news to Davis by offering something positive. We suggested that Davis introduce a bill based on the No Taxation Without Representation Act. This bill would respect the District's borders and provide voting representation through simple legislation under the District Clause of the Constitution. By providing an objective analysis of Davis' idea and offering a concrete way in which he could approach the problem, we took a very big step toward establishing a relationship with Tom Davis and his staff. The next step was to bring together some of our other coalition partners in a meeting with Davis.

While sitting in a semicircle around Tom Davis in his legislative office, the heads of our leading organizations made their case. They were the leaders of Common Cause, DC Appleseed Center, The Leadership Conference on Civil and Human Rights, League of Women Voters of the US, and the NAACP. Tom Davis was delighted to meet with a group of organizations with whom he had had very little previous contact. We assured him at that meeting that if he introduced the bill, we would support him wholeheartedly. Over the course of the next year, we continued to work with Davis, despite the concerns of some Democrats. Consequently, Tom Davis became our lead Republican champion, giving us a bill we could promote as well as bipartisan support, which we had been lacking for about thirty years.

One of the keys to our success with Tom Davis was befriending his very talented committee staff. Key legislative staff give a coalition a direct line to legislators, as well as substantial influence.

Our key staffer was Jim Moore. He served on the House Government Reform Committee. Jim was deeply religious and politically conservative, and he and I disagreed about most other policy questions. The coalition understood at the very outset, however, that Davis would only be as effective as Jim would allow. We decided to see him as a member of the team and set out to win over Jim and other Davis staffers. Jim is a big guy with a big heart and a generous smile. We treated him with respect and trust, and he responded in kind. Jim became a strong believer in representation and DC home rule. His commitment extended well beyond our bill to other critical issues facing the city. Jim became one of the leading DC voting representation experts on the Hill at the time. When Republicans in the Senate were gearing up to oppose us, Jim worked closely with us to develop a written response to the attacks, one that we used and publicized widely. Jim was an essential part of our bipartisan victories. The same is true of Keith Ausbrook, David Marin, and others.

In later years, we recruited other champions. Senator Joe Lieberman aggressively pushed for passage of the bill in the Senate. Delegate Norton had recruited him in 2002. Senator Orrin Hatch was also a vocal champion from 2007 through 2009. Although we had tried to recruit him for several years, we only made progress when we engaged some of our staff allies in the House. Joe Hunter, who was the chief of staff for former Congressman Chris Cannon, worked with a number of Hatch's allies in Utah, who in turn urged the senator to take a leadership role. In this instance, developing a close relationship with congressional staff meant we could expand our base of support. In 2009, we hired Joe to help us work the inside game in Utah.

Additional Stories

During the "Lessons Learned from the Coalition Battlefield" panel discussion, the panelists agreed that champions must be able to cross political party lines while staying "on message." A champion may not be charismatic or ideal, and the champion who rises to the top may not be your first choice, but the champion must believe in the issue and must be able to act genuinely and persuasively when discussing the issue with others.

Bipartisanship is important to maintain when the issue is about fundamental democratic ideals. Sarah Dufendach— who serves as Vice President for Legislative Affairs at Common Cause, an organization advocating good government— recommends paying attention to legislators' speeches in order to find someone who personally cares about the issue.[20] She notes it is better to find a "fiery freshman" to support a campaign than a more senior legislator with less passion for the cause. With the right initial champions, building momentum for cosponsorship and getting support across the aisle can be more readily achieved.

Tanya Clay House, who served as the Director of Public Policy for People For the American Way, adds that while champions can emerge naturally because of a member's personal convictions, at other times, champions may need to be actively educated on an issue and recruited to support it. She advises developing a target list and paying attention to characteristics like committee and subcommittee assignments, caucus leadership, and the strength of home-district constituencies. Several champions, each chosen as effective voices to reach certain communities, may work well. Legislators may be more receptive to the request if it is focused on certain key tasks, rather than leading the entire effort. To be successful at recruiting, House advises being very clear and specific about why the request is being made, exactly what needs to be done, and precisely why the legislator is the best fit for the role. It may not be difficult. House says, "Sometimes members just need to be asked," and are actually quite willing to take part and ally themselves publicly with the issue.

Achieving your goals, however, may require recruiting "strange bedfellows" to get sixty votes in the Senate or a strong majority in other legislatures. For example, Republican Senator John McCain (R-AZ) served as a champion of the Campaign Finance Reform effort, even though he was not at all close to the progressive groups that were pushing that bill. McCain was instrumental in winning valuable Republican support, which led to victory. Common Cause actively recruited McCain. As a champion for the legislation, he was like a rock star because he built excitement for the cause and drew media attention to the issue. As a longtime public servant with a reputation for bucking trends, McCain's support raised the profile on campaign finance and increased its credibility among other GOP senators.

This is a prime example of how you can change the patterns around an issue. McCain became a "container," which focused the media and his colleagues on the bipartisan support for the legislation. Pairing unlikely voices in support of an issue generates more attention, noted Sarah Dufendach. She suggests this technique for getting op-eds placed in local papers. Editorial boards and readers are much more likely to stop and take note when two prominent figures who are not known for agreeing with each other will sign the same letter in support of an issue.

Johnny Barnes, former executive director at the ACLU-National Capital Area Chapter, believes the campaign that passed the DC Voting Rights Constitutional Amendment of 1978 involved several champions. Senator Edward William Brooke III (R-MA) was a champion. Although born, raised, and educated in DC, Brooke couldn't become a US Senator in DC. In 1966, he became the first African-American elected to the US Senate in the ninety-two years since Reconstruction. Senator Ted Kennedy (D-MA) and DC Delegate Walter Fauntroy (D-DC) were also champions of the amendment. Del. Fauntroy deserves the lion's share of the credit for moving the amendment. As a veteran of the Civil Rights Movement, he was instrumental in focusing on legislators who had large concentrations of African-American voters. He secured the support of Senator Strom Thurmond, who once was a vocal segregationist. Like McCain, Fauntroy personally changed the dynamics of the effort. His presence as a container ensured that the focus (i.e., differences) would be around race and civil rights. The communications (i.e., exchanges) he had with others created a significant pattern of change, which dramatically increased support for the amendment. Thus, these champions achieved a tremendous victory in Congress when both chambers passed the constitutional amendment with a two-thirds majority. However, the movement failed to get thirty-eight states to ratify the amendment. See Chapter IV for tips on preparing for what happens after a major victory.

You can always benefit from a champion who is an unusual suspect, like Tom Davis or John McCain, two Republicans who took a lead on issues usually identified with Democrats. At the same time, you should seek out and work with self-selected champions who are naturally identified with your issue because of their state, district, or interest (e.g., DC Delegate Norton fighting for DC voting rights). Ultimately, you will need many champions to succeed.

The Tools: Understanding Patterns in Congress

Under HSD theory, Congress is a "complex adaptive system where semi-autonomous agents interact in unpredictable ways that lead to system-wide patterns."[21] Many books have been written about legislative procedures. Other books focus on how to lobby the Congress (e.g., what to put in information folders, how to prepare for a meeting, whether to send letters electronically, etc.). These books and websites focus on the mechanics of advocacy campaigns. They are very worthwhile and should be a part of any effort to learn how to lobby Congress.[22] My goal here is to give you the tools to navigate through legislative patterns or create new ones.

Legislative champions are essential both because they create a new pattern (when they introduce your bill, get cosponsors, move it through committee) and they understand the patterns of behavior within the Congress that are not fully gleaned from the outside. Patterns include things like the legislative calendar for the year. Typically in Congress, major bills are considered on the floor early in the session, followed by nonbudget bills in the spring, and major appropriations bills in the summer and fall. Under HSD, these patterns are known as periodic attractors: "In a system driven by a periodic attractor, behavior tends to repeat in regular time intervals." [23]

A legislative champion will understand the periodic attractor patterns and know how to use them to your benefit. This person will also know which legislators ought to talk to their colleagues about supporting your bill. A legislator is much more likely to consider supporting your cause if he or she is asked by a trusted colleague. A champion will also know how legislative leaders will respond to pressure from the grassroots and which organizations hold sway over those legislators. Tom Davis repeatedly shared his view that our strongest ally within our coalition was The Leadership Conference on Civil and Human Rights (The Leadership Conference) because ours is a civil rights issue. Once Democrats came to power, that view was reaffirmed by Delegate Eleanor Holmes Norton. She never lost an opportunity to publicly highlight the support and involvement of The Leadership Conference. Consequently, we made sure that they were our lead advocates on the Hill.

Legislative champions also create patterns of behavior based on their position. Legislators are more likely to support a chairman's bill than they would legislation introduced by a junior legislator. In fact, in 2007, twenty-two Republicans voted for the DC Voting Rights Act in the House. Tom Davis attributed more than half those votes to his chairmanship of the House Government Reform Committee the year before. While over a dozen of those members either left the Congress or were defeated by 2008, two of them changed their stance after Tom Davis retired. Darrell Issa decided to oppose our bill and Mike Pence decided to lower his profile. Davis, under HSD tools, is a point attractor. HSD Founder Glenda Eoyang said, "In a point attractor system, all activities in the system tend toward a single point." [24] Point attractors, by their very nature, create patterns around them. Once the point attractor is gone (i.e., retires), the pattern shifts.

Legislative champions are also drawn to causes that gain steam. They often see patterns emerging in the country at large, in their legislative districts, or on a particular issue. One Senate Democratic aide said of a senator: "He figures out what the wave is and then he gets on top of it." [25]

Give people the ability to create a "wave." You will likely draw the attention and support of additional legislative champions who want to be point attractors.

The Bottom Line

1. All legislative efforts are dependent on legislative champions taking up your cause and doing the hard work to get the bill passed.

2. Find the right champion by figuring out which legislative committee has jurisdiction over your issue.

3. Try to interest the person who is both passionate about your issue and has power (e.g., the person who has seniority and perhaps is chair or ranking legislator).

4. When you find your champion(s), remember that the staff plays a pivotal role in how effective you will be; therefore, cultivate a relationship of trust with the champion's staff and stay in frequent contact.

5. Your champion will help you understand the patterns at work, and use those patterns to your advantage.

III. Secure Votes by Avoiding Extremes

Get a jump on the legislative process by starting with the bill that you believe will engender broad support and is most likely to pass.

The Story

"You should fight for your principles and leave the compromises to us," a Democratic congressman told representatives from our coalition during a meeting in the fall of 2006.[26] The Republicans were in control of the House. Our goal at the meeting was to get the congressman to support a compromise bill, one that would provide a House seat for DC residents and an additional seat for the State of Utah (which had barely missed getting a fourth seat after the 2000 census). The congressman's response was not a surprise. In fact, most public interest advocates believe that the way to move a bill through the Congress is to focus on everything you want, and then back down over time to a compromise bill that is achievable.

But in the case of DC Vote, activists have been fighting for forty years. They tried a constitutional amendment. They tried to create a state of New Columbia. None of that worked. So if we started with a full representation bill or a statehood bill, we could have gotten the congressman to support it, but other members of Congress would not have viewed our issue, or the bill, as something they had to seriously consider. In fact, that was the situation DC Vote was facing while trying to drum up support for Del. Norton's No Taxation

Without Representation Act that called for full voting representation in both the House and the Senate. We would be one of those thousands of bills introduced every year— over 10,000 in the 109th Congress and over 11,100 in the 110th— that make people feel good, but don't go anywhere.[27] These bills stay in the UnOrganized Zone without hearings, committee votes, or floor action (see Introduction). Only around ten percent of introduced bills are ever taken up for any further action by either chamber.[28]

There are times when you want to protect a policy or program (like job training programs or an environmental regulation), or define a political fight with enough clarity so that you "win" the message war. The latter fights generally involve major public policy debates where both sides have a great deal at stake, such as ending tax breaks for corporations, expanding entitlement programs, or ending military engagements abroad. During these types of advocacy campaigns, it may make sense to use the outside game to push for everything you want as a way to sway public opinion and/or media coverage, and thereby arm your allies during tough negotiations in Congress. The 112th Congress essentially consisted of major message fights between Republicans who sought to cut domestic spending and Democrats who wanted to increase taxes on the super rich.

Although major policy disputes dominate our news cycles, most organizations are working toward more modest changes in public policy. In these situations, if you want to command serious attention and get people invested in working to turn your idea into the law of the land (i.e., creating movement out of the Unorganized and into the Self-Organizing Zone), you have to start with a viable bill. For it to be viable, it should engender bipartisan support whenever possible.[29]

We knew Tom Davis did not support representation in the Senate. "I think this theory works specifically for the House, but not for the Senate," Davis said to us during one of our meetings. "Representation in the Senate is much more closely aligned with the status of a state." None of us on the activist side believed that. In fact, our ultimate goal was to get representation in the Senate. But our coalition had to focus on only getting a representative in the House so that we could secure enough support especially in the Senate, where you need sixty votes to prevent a filibuster and get an agreement between the majority and the minority to avoid countless hours of debate.[30]

To attract bipartisan support, we embraced a compromise that would provide representation for DC residents in the House of Representatives as a first step to full democracy. By doing so, we increased agreement among our coalition and moved into the Self-Organizing Zone. We would achieve the goal of getting representation in the House by expanding the size of the House by two, with one seat going to DC and the other for the next state eligible. We made the expansion permanent in order to secure the support of Democratic House members in the Midwest, who were fearful that their states would lose a seat if our bill became law. Utah was the next state eligible, which made this bill attractive to us. As one of the most Republican states, Utah was a terrific balance to DC, the most Democratic jurisdiction in America. We also embraced a novel legal theory that Congress could, by simple legislation, provide representation for DC residents. We did that for two overriding reasons. First, we did not have the votes to pass a constitutional amendment or to secure statehood. Second, we could not get any traction in Congress unless members believed that the bill they were promoting was actually achievable.

We decided to call the bill the DC Voting Rights Act (eventually Delegate Norton used this name as the official title of the bill). With this name, we built a strong "container." Our goal was to align ourselves the positive feelings in Congress associated with the Voting Rights Act and the civil rights movement of the 1960s. Additionally, we wanted to use language that would resonate around the country. The polls and focus groups we commissioned demonstrated very clearly that Americans respond favorably to the idea that DC residents deserve equal voting rights. All of these adaptive changes helped us move firmly into the Organized Zone of the Landscape Diagram where there was more agreement about the components of the bill and more certainty among leaders about moving it (see Introduction).

After the Democrats swept the White House and the Congress in 2008, we held a series of meetings with our Board of Directors, our coalition partners, and supporters to decide which bill we would promote in this (short) period of progressive "change." A lot of people were inclined to do what the congressman had suggested a few years before—publicly back the strongest bill possible, and compromise along the way. Our question during those sessions was, "Which bill is most likely to pass?" We asked that question because we were seeking the option that created the most agreement and certainty. In early 2009, Democrats had fifty-eight seats.[31] Two Democrats, Max Baucus, and Robert Byrd opposed our bill. So that meant that we needed some Republican support to get to sixty votes. That was true even in a year when Barack Obama became president and "change" was sweeping Washington. During those meetings, most people expressed support for full representation, or even statehood. But when framed this way, the answer became clear: we had to support the DC Voting Rights Act (i.e., the DC-Utah compromise).

The 111th Congress took up the DC voting rights bill within the first months of the new year because we supported, once again, the same bipartisan bill that previously moved through the House and the Senate. We had a leg up to pass our bill because we started with a bipartisan compromise. More importantly, when the bill got to the Senate, we had the Republican votes needed to prevent a filibuster. In fact, Republican votes made all the difference. On February 24, 2009, sixty-two senators voted for cloture on the Motion to Proceed (which allows the Senate to consider a bill).[32] Seven of those votes were from Republicans.[33] After considerable debate and votes on amendments, sixty-one Senators voted to pass the DC VRA.

Additional Stories

Joshua Horwitz, the executive director at the Coalition to Stop Gun Violence, comprised of forty-eight national organizations, emphasizes that attracting bipartisan supporters is essential.[34] Enlisting leaders from outside the traditional core of your Hill support— those whose names have long been associated with your cause— will expand a campaign's influence in new directions. His coalition had long counted on support from leaders like Senator Harry Reid (D-NV) and Senator Diane Feinstein (D-CA), but they focused on cross-aisle support as well and did succeed in involving Rep. Tom Davis. However, Horwitz notes that over his twenty years in reform advocacy, bipartisan support is growing harder to achieve, with the atmosphere more polarized, and the Democratic Party split internally over certain controversial issues like gun safety laws. In comparison to years past, he sees fewer centrist Republicans left in office on the Hill and, therefore, fewer opportunities to build constructive relationships with moderates across the aisle.

Nancy Zirkin, executive vice president at the Leadership Conference on Civil and Human Rights, the nation's oldest and largest civil rights coalition, agrees that bipartisan inclusion is important.[35] She notes that the efforts she was involved in to move disability legislation in 2008 were successful because the complex details of the legislation were negotiated ahead of time with input from all sides. Involving legislators of both parties in early discussions on legislative proposals will increase the possibilities for support later on in the process.

The Tools: Soften Your Boundaries by Choosing Bills Wisely

We all know from personal experience that people find comfort in repetition and in the familiar. That is true even when the patterns of behavior have a negative consequence. Most people cannot recognize the pattern itself, and therefore find it difficult to modify their behavior.

Lines in the sand get drawn very early in Congress, especially around partisan legislation. Legislation (which is a "container") creates very specific differences and exchanges among the people who care about your issue. When advocacy groups promote "purist" bills, they will often push certain legislators to stake out public positions in opposition to the bill. The bills, in effect, create distinct boundaries between Democrats and Republicans (see Chapter VII for a description of boundaries). Additionally, if a purist bill is moved through the committee and floor without much change (based on the idea that the other chamber of Congress will fix it or that it will be fixed in conference between the two chambers), members of Congress who might be inclined to support a compromise bill will be forced into a negative vote.

Here's what Senator Kent Conrad said about his decision to not hold a mark-up of a budget bill in 2011: "If you go through a partisan markup, it hardens people's positions and makes it more difficult to get a bipartisan agreement."[36]

It is much harder to get a legislator to change a vote than it is to get him or her to support a compromise. On the other hand, you will be forced to compromise as a bill winds through the legislative process. So, ask for a little bit more than you expect, knowing that you will have to give some in the end. Achieving this balance is difficult, but very necessary. Rely on your legislative champions and the experienced members of your coalition to figure out whether you have achieved the right balance.

The DC VRA represents our effort to find a compromise bill. It provided an additional seat for both parties, so it was vote neutral. It addressed neither representation in the Senate, nor local control issues. Yet, Norton had left some areas where we could "give in," such as agreeing to expedited judicial review of the bill and a provision declaring that the bill did not apply to Senate representation.

Another example of this dynamic is the health care reform fight of the early 1990s. The Clinton Administration pursued a sweeping universal healthcare plan. They presented it to Congress, promoted the bill, and vigorously opposed any compromise. Republican opponents offered an alternative bill that was also sweeping in the changes it would achieve (in fact, it was very similar to the bill Democrats enacted in 2010). But the patterns of behavior for and against the Clinton bill were formed. The early opportunity for compromise disappeared. Republicans opposed the Clinton bill, ensuring that Democrats could not get sixty votes in the Senate. Health care reform died that year as a result. Congress would wait another sixteen years before considering healthcare reform again.

The Tools: Adaptive Action

The Adaptive Action tool is especially useful when deciding how to keep your issue and legislation bipartisan. Here's the tool:

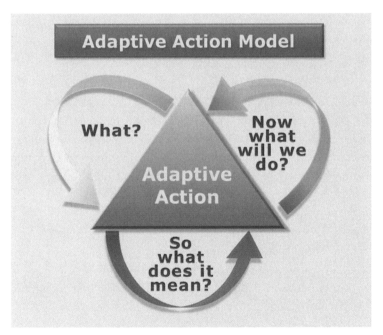

Diagram 3: Adaptive Action Model

You can use the "what, so what, and now what" questions embodied in this tool for most of the chapters in this book. Some relevant questions that you might want to ask yourself when thinking about your bill are:

- What is the problem you are trying to fix?
- What would your fix mean to your supporters in Congress?
- What would your fix mean to people who oppose you?
- Are there changes you can make at the outset that might turn some erstwhile opponents into supporters?
- What would that compromise look like?
- What would it mean for your coalition and constituency?
- Based on those answers, now what will you do?

You can see the cycle of questions here. Every compromise or solution to a problem creates another round of adaptive questions. By addressing these questions head-on, you can discover which legislative changes will attract bipartisan support while keeping the container of your coalition and the core goal of your legislation intact.

Use the Adaptive Action Model while you are developing your bill and searching for co-sponsorship and support.

The Bottom Line

1. Understand that your bill will create patterns of behavior in Congress that will be hard to change later.

2. Where possible, begin the legislative process by recruiting bipartisan and/or broad support at the outset before your bill is created.

3. To secure enough votes, develop a bill that will attract a range of legislative champions and thus significantly increase your chances of success.

4. Use the Adaptive Action Model at each stage of bill development.

IV. Lead a Working Coalition

Create or Join a coalition of organizations with a common interest and enable them to magnify your collective power.

The Story

I sat at our conference table with a representative from Common Cause, staring at the clock. We were supposed to be holding a meeting of our coalition partners. Three months earlier, we met with over twenty people at our office at 1500 U Street. Now there were just two of us. I could barely conceal my profound disappointment.

DC Vote decided early on that we would run a national campaign and engage people around the country by creating a coalition of organizations. We would ask our coalition partners to engage their members by first educating them and then by asking them to urge their representatives in Congress to support DC voting rights. We would also use these organizations to help us gather intelligence on Capitol Hill through their contacts. Lastly, we would maximize their political strength by asking them to attend meetings, cosign letters, and generate votes in Congress. Indeed, a few of the legislative aides I interviewed said that letters from coalitions and organizations were much more valued than individual letters from constituents. The reason for this is that organizations represent many people and have the institutional capacity to generate news, and even promote or defeat a candidate for office.

Back when we were primarily focused on educating people about DC's status, our coalition partners told us that they needed more than an educational mandate: they needed a bill around which to engage their grassroots members. So, that's what we came up with. But I was finding it very difficult to get our coalition working in early 2005. A major reason for the inaction was that little was happening on Capitol Hill.

Rep. Tom Davis had not made much headway in recruiting other Republicans to support the DC Voting Rights Act. Additionally, Davis had not held a hearing or markup yet that year. So, after that disappointing meeting in our office, I decided to change the container (i.e., venue) for our monthly meetings. I asked Jim Moore if he would be willing to host the meetings up on the Hill. I thought that he and other Davis staffers would feel more pressure to accomplish something before these meetings in order to have some activity to report. I also thought that coalition partners would want to come to Hill meetings because they would assume that there was movement taking place. I expected that they, too, would feel pressured to report on their activities and would, therefore, do some work before each meeting.

The tactic worked. We had nearly twenty people at our next meeting in July of 2005. Within a matter of weeks, organizations were taking action, as was Tom Davis. In August of that year, Common Cause sent an action alert to over 250,000 people nationwide. Also that month, nineteen coalition groups cosigned a letter to Senator Mike DeWine (R-OH), and the US League of Women Voters spearheaded the follow-up to seek his sponsorship of a DC voting rights bill.

DC Vote's role in the coalition was to draft plans for action, facilitate agreement on the best plans, implement the areas where we assumed responsibility, and provide assistance to the other organizations in implementing their part of the plan. At DC Vote, we like to describe our role as the center of the wheel: our coalition partners are the spokes and together we move faster toward our goals.

If you are joining or forming a coalition that will likely work together over many years to address a seemingly intractable problem, the coalition should either create a formal organization (with staff and other resources) which the coalition controls through the Board of Directors and task forces, or empower one of the organizations to serve as the facilitator of a more informal "coalition of the willing."

The Leadership Conference on Civil and Human Rights is an excellent example of a formal organization created by other groups which expected to work together on civil rights causes over many decades. The Leadership Conference was founded in 1950 by A. Philip Randolph, head of the Brotherhood of Sleeping Car Porters; Roy Wilkins of the National Association for the Advancement of Colored People; and Arnold Aronson, a leader of the National Jewish Community Relations Advisory Council. It is a formal coalition where every one of the over-200 members is on the board of directors. Each organization pays annual dues. The Executive Committee of their Board is comprised of over thirty organizations with the power to hire or fire the president. The Leadership Conference has roughly fifteen task forces that develop and implement action plans. While the organization does not have written principles, they do have established positions that serve as the "common law" of the coalition. Moreover, The Leadership Conference operates by consensus. Where they do not have consensus, such as on issues like campaign finance or abortion, they do not act. If any organization is opposed to a position of The Leadership Conference, they can force a formal vote on whether or not to change that position. This option is so rarely used, however, that current CEO and President Wade Henderson cannot remember when such a vote has ever been taken.

The DC Voting Rights Coalition is an excellent example of a more informal, ad hoc coalition. In our case, we bring together a "coalition of the willing." We, too, operate by consensus. Organizations can and do object to some of our collective positions. But, unless that objection is shared by a large majority of our coalition, we proceed. Objecting organizations may then decide not to participate in part of our activities, or leave the coalition entirely. Additionally, some of our partners are interested in working on representation in Congress and not local democracy.

In an informal coalition, the facilitating organization can be the one that is closest to the issue or has the resources to devote to managing the coalition and facilitating its work. DC voting rights is the heart and soul of what DC Vote does as an organization. In fact, during the first ten years, we focused almost exclusively on DC representation in Congress. The other members of the coalition care very much about DC voting rights, but it is only one of the issues that they work on. They are busy and want to help the cause as quickly and efficiently as possible by maximizing their assistance in a minimal amount of time. DC Vote also has a board of directors that is comprised of individuals not associated with our coalition partners. So, our partners do not have the power to hire or fire the executive director or to decide the ultimate direction of the organization.

In both formal and informal coalitions, members need to have the opportunity for significant input in the decision-making and execution process for the coalition to succeed. They need to give voice to their ideas and concerns, and shape the coalition strategy. Effective coalitions, therefore, provide multiple opportunities for members of the coalition to affect the policies and positions of the coalition, as well as implement the strategy.

In the first few years of the DC Vote coalition, we kept the decision-making process to the core group of organizations that had first joined. Within DC Vote, we called this group the strategic planning committee. Formal coalitions have this type of structure as well. DC Vote selected members of the committee, organized the calls, and set the agenda. That process worked well for a while. Then the National Urban League, People for the American Way, and others emerged as leaders within the coalition. That meant that we had to empower the broader coalition to weigh in on questions we were considering and to take a leadership role in implementing our decisions.

We began a process in 2008 to ensure that our coalition reflected the vision of our partners. We held a roundtable discussion with subgroups. Meetings of the larger group followed those sessions where we resolved important decisions, particularly whether we would shift our focus after Barack Obama won the election and Democrats in the Congress increased their margin. The answer was no; we would keep pushing the DC VRA. The rationale was simple: our best chance of getting a bill signed into law was to push for passage of the DC VRA. If we had championed a new bill, we would have chosen a new container and shifted all the patterns we had developed, resulting in a new bill with additional hearings, new sponsors, shifting alliances, and the need to educate a bunch of people (in DC, the media, the Hill, etc.) about an entirely new bill (see Diagram 2).

A more formal process may work better for other coalitions (see below for Additional Stories). Whatever approach you take, make sure that it reflects a group decision that is explicit and supported by the coalition members.

Additional Stories

One advocate describes the best coalitions as those which know what the goal is and appreciate the value of each member organization in reaching it. She laments that too many coalitions with worthy goals stumble over internal personality conflicts and turf wars when multiple groups compete over taking— or keeping— a lead role. This is especially damaging, she notes, if the Hill staff with whom the coalition is working get a sense that there is discord or uncertainty in the coalition, since it can erode the perceived value of the coalition as a partner in the policy effort. In her view, well-run coalitions need a strong sense of respect for the potential of each group to take the lead in certain areas, depending on which voice will be most effective with which audiences. Members also need an understanding that consensus decisions are important, but consensus does not mean that all groups will agree with every aspect and unanimously sign all letters or endorse all steps. Oftentimes, a coalition will need to move forward without unanimity.

Another advocate suggests coalitions adopt a structure with both a core group willing to devote more time and staff, and a wider supporting group to lend strength and credibility to a campaign (much like the DC voting rights coalition). The smaller group can staff task forces that meet and decide on next steps, while the wider group engages by signing letters and activating its members. This works best if a general consensus can be initially agreed on. It can be developed into a guiding document that represents the coalition's principles, particularly its funding and financing arrangements, to prevent misunderstandings.

One veteran leader of coalitions similarly emphasizes that while core leader groups are necessary, the lead group must seek input and act transparently. In order to be successful, "every group has to feel that what's happening benefits them and the issue and that they have a voice and a say," she explains.

No matter what size the coalition, one experienced public interest lobbyist said, leaders have to focus on "using people's time efficiently" and running effective meetings. "Washington coalitions are especially bad at this," she said. She advised that leaders need to figure out which of the participating organizations and individuals are really invested and therefore need to feel the most included, and which will be content to be notified rather than take part in every decision. Paying attention to these dynamics, she said, may help prevent the "worst part of coalition politics," when the group is divided over critical decisions and may become a "circular firing squad."

Our panelists from the Lessons Learned from the Coalition Battlefield meeting we held in 2002 agreed that coalitions should establish general agreements on principles that are shared by as many parts of the coalition as possible. Remember, while everyone is riding the same train with a specific destination in mind, not everyone in the coalition will get on or off at the same stop. Some organizations will leave the coalition when you make compromises along the way. Other groups may join your coalition because of those compromises or when you are closer to your destination.

The campaign for the Family and Medical Leave Act of 1993 showed that it can be important to have the national coalition of organizations based in Washington mirror the local coalition based in the states in order to aid mobilizing efforts. Labor organizations were needed partners in the campaign. As other parts of the coalition became more visible and demonstrated political power, labor took the issue more seriously and joined the effort.

Sometimes the effort expended to fuse together unlikely groups can help greatly enhance the strength of a movement. For the Family and Medical Leave Act Campaign, Meredith McGhee reports that the US Catholic Conference and anti-abortion organizations worked together with pro-choice organizations to bring strength to the campaign that would not have been found elsewhere. The various organizations obviously had different reasons for working on the issue, but they all supported family and medical leave in spite of those differences.

The Tools: Use the CDE Model to Understand and Influence Your Coalition

Containers help to define organizations and the focus of their work (see Chapter I, Diagram 2). Organizational containers are what we think of as giving form to our ideas and missions. Conceptual containers are ideological.[37] DC Vote is an example of an organizational container. Within that container lies DC Vote's mission— fighting for voting representation in Congress, which is an ideological container.

Choosing the right container is critical for more than just framing an issue. Prior to 2002, DC Vote was not a fully developed organization. It had poorly functioning containers. There were volunteer-led committees tasked with doing core organizational work. They had a focus on educating people about DC's disenfranchisement and the possible solutions, and not on advocating for a specific solution. While the volunteer engagement meant greater grassroots ownership, many of the core functions of an organization (bookkeeping, fundraising, relationship building, all of which can be seen as "exchanges" within the CDE) were not fully being fulfilled. So, our container limited the differences that were expressed. Also, by defining DC Vote's primary objective (container) as a vehicle for education rather than for a specific legislative outcome, the differences and exchanges were around which theoretical solution would be best, rather than how to move specific legislation. Therefore, the DC democracy movement at that point was rudderless.

We significantly changed the containers of our organization in 2002. We built a more traditional organization led by professional employees. Additionally, we decided to embrace specific legislative goals. The difference was dramatic. Within a few years, we quadrupled the size of our staff, budget, and coalition. With a much larger coalition, in 2007 we secured a majority vote in the House and Senate for a DC Voting Rights bill for the first time in a generation (although a filibuster in the Senate prevented Congress from passing the bill).

Differences create the potential for movement or change across the coalition. Therefore, it is important to always seek diversity and allow people to share their views. When evaluating how effective your coalition is, ask how much difference of opinion or experiences you allow, or cultivate, at meetings. At the DC Voting Rights Coalition, we routinely asked people to react to suggestions, ideas, or activities. For some time, many of our partners chose to keep their differences to themselves to facilitate getting through the agenda. This low difference, low exchange approach can be helpful when you are mostly in agreement about your advocacy goals and the tactics you are employing to further those goals. But, because the exchange level is low, high differences can also exist beneath the surface. This situation can lead to uncoupling, or fracturing, of your coalition.

The Decision Matrix is an excellent model for you to use when you are trying to figure out the existing or desirable level of engagement and activity of your coalition.

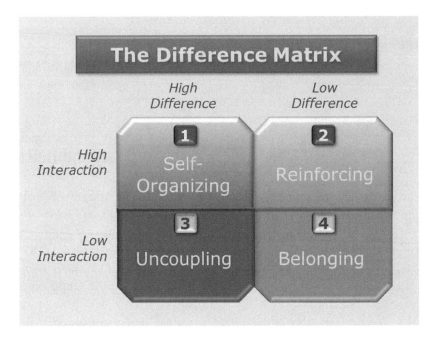

Diagram 4: The Difference Matrix

As Glenda Eoyang (HSD founder) would say, none of these places on the model are "naughty or nice" (i.e., intrinsically preferable). Many coalition members praised us when the meetings were low-interaction affairs that exposed few differences. In their view, we were using our meetings effectively by getting through the agenda and keeping everyone focused on the work at hand. Of course, with low exchanges, you can never be sure if people were masking their differences. It is also true that when groups have high exchanges of ideas and high differences, as long as they resolve their differences in a productive way, the individual organizations also have greater ownership and engage in more activity. Of course, you cannot stay in this place too long, otherwise conflicts will emerge, potentially leading to low exchanges, high differences, and uncoupling.

You need to determine where your coalition stands in the matrix and where you want it to be. Use the Adaptive Action Model (see Chapter III) to figure out your next steps.

Within the DC Voting Rights Coalition, we sought more ideas and a greater understanding of our coalition's views when differences were not being expressed. That was especially true when the prospects of a bill moving through the Congress looked bleak. We needed to develop programs to increase grassroots engagement. We created committees to brainstorm ideas and report back. Under HSD models, such a committee can be considered a container. You have to decide how narrow or broad a task you assign to a committee. A broad mandate (e.g., think about how we get this bill through Congress) would expose many differences, resulting in significant exchanges of ideas, and, therefore, many recommendations to the coalition. On the other hand, a narrow mandate (e.g., figure out which members of the committee might be opposed to our bill) would limit the differences of opinions shared by the participants, while also narrowing the number of possible outcomes.

You should figure out beforehand the result you are seeking, and structure the mandate accordingly.

Let's add the CDE to the Landscape Diagram.

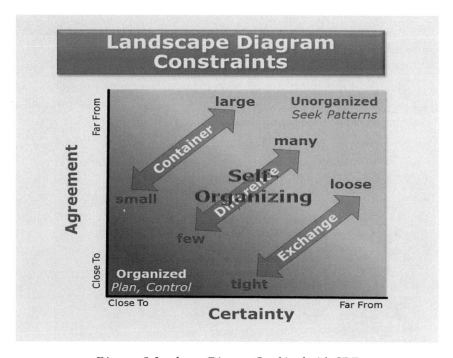

Diagram 5: Landscape Diagram Combined with CDE

You can see how, by varying the constraints, you can move patterns through the zones. By narrowing the container, differences, and exchanges, you increase certainty and agreement because there are fewer opportunities for people to disagree. Just regulate that by narrowing the discussion, you will reduce both the range of information you receive and the number of creative ideas presented. The trick is understanding the appropriate moment when you want to move toward that left bottom corner and need to constrain the choices and discussion within your coalition.

The Bottom Line

1. Broad, national coalitions are needed to popularize the issue, to capture the attention of the media, and to attract champions. Just as important—they are necessary to do advocacy legwork.

2. Coalitions help you target specific districts and/or constituencies by asking people to contact their legislators.

3. Expect different levels of commitment and engagement from different coalition members based on their capacity and commitment to the coalition's mission.

4. Coalitions require ongoing efforts and hard work to keep the movement alive, even when there is no legislative action.

5. Use the HSD models to decide your appropriate container and the degree of differences you want to encourage within your coalition.

V. Empower the Grassroots

When people fight for their rights, they create energy that is critical to your mission.

The Story

They asked me to keep the people home. The House Government Reform Committee was holding a markup of the DC House Voting Rights Act in 2006, and some thought that Republicans might be more likely to vote against the bill if there were a lot of DC residents there. I listened patiently. I understood their point. We were courting Republicans, who were in the majority. There are some Republicans who loathe the District. Perhaps having lots of Washingtonians breathing down their necks might make some of our Republican supporters second-guess their "commitment" to our bill.

We believed, however, that we could change the dynamics in the room precisely by asking lots of folks to show up. Whenever there was action on our issue, we put out the word to our volunteers and coalition partners. We also urged the reform committee to set up a separate viewing area for the overflow crowd. Hundreds of people showed up for the markup on May 18, 2006. The atmosphere was electrifying. In fact, former Secretary Jack Kemp came as well. He was energized as he walked into the back room of the committee chambers. There he found Congressman Dan Burton and began discussing the bill with him. Burton (R-IN), just minutes before, had expressed his opposition to the

35

bill in very strong terms. I believe the mood at the markup, as reflected in Jack Kemp's presentation to Burton in the back chambers, helped to change his mind.[38] Within minutes, Burton came out and announced that, for the first time in his career, he was switching his vote and declared: "'I'd like to say we should support this as a civil rights step.'"[39] Burton caught us totally by surprise. We thought he would remain one of our fiercest opponents. The packed chambers also energized our Democratic supporters on the committee by demonstrating to them that DC residents cared. Lastly, the large crowd added to the significance of the event, which led the *Washington Post* to place a story about the markup on the front page.[40] As in nature, small changes can have huge consequences. In this case, the electrifying energy in the room had a huge impact on Rep. Burton, and others.

At a dinner a few months after Burton's conversion, former Senator John Breaux (D-LA) told me "no one from Louisiana ever asked me to support DC voting rights when I was in the Senate." We were meeting at an event hosted by DC resident Jeff Zients, at the urging of political commentator Mark Plotkin. I had heard this complaint before. Of course, legislators respond first and foremost to their constituents. One of our major questions, as we formulated a strategy in 2002 was, how do we get Americans outside of DC to help us?

There are a wide range of options available for engaging people outside your jurisdiction. They include contacting friends and family in other states, creating embarrassing situations for elected officials that garner press attention in their states, attending marches that lead to news stories, proposing creative ideas like adding a new slogan to a license plate, and so forth.

DC Vote spent years collecting petition signatures from Washingtonians who attended Adams Morgan, Black Luv, Pride, and other local festivals. These folks were our strongest supporters, the base of the movement. Not only did they attend markups and hearings, they also called their friends and family members outside DC to enlist their help. In 2007, we needed that help to persuade three moderate Republican Senators from the Homeland Security Committee to support our bill. Senate Democrats, at the time, had forty-nine seats. Senate Republicans had forty-nine seats. There were two independents that caucused with the Democrats. Our goal was to get sixty senators to support our bill so that we could prevent a filibuster. The key was first getting the three moderate Republicans: Susan Collins (R-ME), George Voinovich (R-OH), and Norm Coleman (R-MN).

During the early years of our fight, we launched advocacy drives we called Operation Ohio, Operation Maine, etc. We asked DC residents to contact their family and friends in those states to get those people to contact their Senators. We also asked our coalition partners to engage their members within these states. Senator Susan Collins reported to her colleagues and also to the assembled audience at the Senate markup that she had indeed heard from a lot of her constituents. The same was true of the Senators from Ohio and Minnesota. In fact, we generated phone calls to those offices in advance of the mark-up by the Senate Homeland Security and Governmental Affairs Committee. We also worked the inside game with her and others by getting their donors, DC officials, former Republican legislators, and others to contact them directly.

The results were encouraging. Collins became a strong supporter of the bill, and both Coleman and Voinovich gave passionate statements in its favor before voting to support the bill during a markup on June 13, 2007. The vote at the Senate Homeland Committee meeting was 9-1.[41]

Senator George Voinovich's (R-OH) yes vote that day was a direct result of an action by DC residents years earlier. In 2005, DC shadow Senator Paul Strauss organized a group of activists for a boat excursion. The Organization for Security and Cooperation in Europe was meeting in Washington, DC over the July Fourth weekend. A group of US Senators and Representatives were participating in the meeting as well. We got word that a delegation was taking a boat trip down the Potomac River. Strauss and his group followed them on the boat, holding up signs demanding a vote in Congress.[42] Senator George Voinovich (R-OH) was on that boat. Over the next few years, every time he explained why he supports DC voting rights legislation, he cited his embarrassment that day when he had to explain to visiting dignitaries why Washingtonians were disenfranchised.

We also sought ways to support people who had innovative ideas. For example, DC Vote embraced an idea by DC resident Sarah Shapiro, a summer intern, to add the slogan "taxation without representation" to DC's license plates. She had mentioned the idea on the Mark Plotkin radio program. Mark then championed the cause. DC Vote helped out by lobbying the DC City Council and Mayor Anthony Williams, who, reluctantly, signed into law a bill doing exactly what Sarah suggested. This is an excellent example of how a lone activist can have a dramatic impact when an advocacy organization is eager to support people taking action.

Sarah's suggestion ultimately resulted in millions of license plates over the past ten years traveling around the Washington metropolitan area and throughout the country with our slogan on them. President Clinton put the license plate on the presidential limousine prior to his departure in December 2000, and President Bush promptly removed them in January 2001. President Obama chose not to put them back on the presidential vehicles. Each time a president did something with the license plates, the national and international media ran news stories on our issue. Countless Americans have learned about the District's plight as a result of those license plates.

Additionally, the slogan on the license plates had an effect on the Hill. At a Judiciary Committee hearing on January 27, 2009, Rep. Louis Gohmert, a Texas Republican who is fiercely opposed to DC voting rights, said: "Who ever came up with the idea to put 'taxation without representation' on the DC license plates, it's worked. It has made an impact on me."[43] Gohmert proposed legislation to eliminate federal income taxes for DC residents until they get representation.[44]

Many people on the Hill are often dismissive of rallies, arguing that advocates ought to focus on having direct contact with legislators. When one leads to the other, however, mass protests can be extremely effective. For instance, activists for gay rights were divided over the wisdom of a march on Washington in October 2009. *The New York Times* quoted Representative Barney Frank, the highest-ranking, openly gay official in US politics, as saying "of their intention to pressure the Obama administration, 'The only thing they're going to put pressure on is the grass.'"[45] He was also quoted in *The Washington Post* describing the march as "useless."[46] Yet major newspapers covered the event, along with accounts of President Obama's appearance at the Human Rights Campaign (a gay rights group), where he pledged to repeal the ban on gays serving in America's armed services.

When marches raise an issue's profile— because of a large turnout, media coverage, and/or comments by elected officials—they can be an effective tactic. In fact, by March 2010, the Pentagon took major steps to restrict the enforcement of the "Don't Ask, Don't Tell" policy. Moreover, Admiral Mike Mullen, the Chair of Joint Chiefs of Staff, called on Congress to change the law. Senator Joe Lieberman and others responded by introducing repeal legislation. In the ensuing months, gay rights activists chained themselves to the White House fence, shouted down Democratic leaders at events, and put considerable pressure on the Congress. In December 2010, Congress passed a bill repealing "Don't Ask, Don't Tell," and President Barack Obama signed it into law.

Similarly, DC Vote staged a voting rights march on April 16, 2007 that drew national attention. Five thousand DC residents showed up on a cold, windy day. The entire City Council and Mayor Adrian Fenty were in attendance. NBC, the *PBS News Hour*, Associated Press, and others did stories on the march that were carried nationally. Locally, the *Washington Post* covered the march extensively, as did all the area television, radio, and print media. A week after the march, the House considered and passed a DC voting rights bill.

This is a grassroots campaign in action— switching votes, convincing elected officials who are ambivalent, creating news stories, securing policy promises from a president, and influencing a change in policy and the law. Our job as advocacy organizations is to provide opportunities for people to fight for their rights.

Additional Stories

Nancy Zirkin, Executive Vice-President of the Leadership Conference on Civil and Human Rights, stresses that effective campaigns include a multitiered strategy for activism. It is important to find many voices to carry the message. Organizations must mobilize, not only voices that legislators listen to, like people they know, but lots of different voices from their constituency as well. Depending on the legislators you are trying to influence, the most essential voices could be labor leaders, business leaders, university presidents, older voters, or other respected residents in the constituent community.

Noah T. Winer, formerly of MoveOn, says "people enjoy doing things that they feel are effective." Founded in 1998 and with over five million members, MoveOn uses a consultation process that includes rounds of e-mail polls and surveys of members, allowing them to vote on priorities and express their level of interest in a variety of current events.[47] Winer notes that the organization also routinely sends out surveys to 10,000 randomly selected members to understand their views and gauge approval of the organization's activities. In addition, he explains that it is less about the specific activity and more about the opportunity to make an impact. Winer says successful organizations "tell a credible story" to their volunteers about what they are being asked to do, how the organization can succeed with their help, and what will happen if they don't take action. "When that picture is clear," Winer says, "then people are the most excited to engage."

Meredith McGehee, of Campaign Legal Center, similarly emphasizes developing a focused, specific message that citizen activists can be comfortable delivering and, therefore, it can become more effective. The overall goal is to help the grassroots send a "meaningful message at the appropriate moment." Often, she says, people find the idea of meeting with a legislator to be very threatening; volunteers may not have been active in politics at all before. A focused message with only two or three talking points can be very helpful to enable a successful interaction for your cause. For example, our citizen-activists often talked about DC residents serving in the armed forces abroad to protect our democracy without enjoying full democracy here at home.

Sometimes a message just doesn't get through or a traditional advocacy campaign isn't successful because the affected population is too disempowered and marginalized. In those cases, you may need to consider more direct-action tactics and even civil disobedience.

"Direct action" can be defined as an advocacy tactic where you confront your opponents in ways that make them feel uncomfortable because you violate a cultural norm or unspoken rule. Examples include DC Vote holding a prayer vigil in Senator John Tester's (D-MT) office. He introduced a bill in 2010 that would wipe away the District's gun laws. We wanted to challenge him in person in front of the media. So, we staged a "pray in" in his office with a few DC clergy. We demanded to see Tester. When his staff told us that he wasn't available but they could try to schedule us in, we told them we would pray in his office until he showed up. Sure enough, forty-five minutes later he showed up. Our exchange with him made the news in DC and Montana, and our forceful tactic buoyed our supporters.[48] Direct action aims to elicit a public response from the target that is reported in the media. That was the result of our "pray in," making the tactic successful. Tester also decided not to push for enactment of his gun bill, providing us with a major victory.

Civil disobedience can be defined as repeated acts that violate a specific law, leading to arrests and a crisis that must be resolved, hopefully in the advocate's favor. Media coverage is a secondary goal in civil disobedience. The civil rights movement of the 1950s and 1960s and the Free South Africa movement of the 1980s are excellent examples of successful civil disobedience campaigns.[49] DC Vote adopted a civil disobedience campaign in 2011 after the DC VRA stalled and Republicans began trying to chip away at DC's home rule authority. See Chapter X for a further discussion.

The Tools: Recognizing the Role of "Voice"

Human systems are entirely dependent on "voice"— people sharing their opinions, their fears, their desires, their aspirations, and so forth. As we saw above, organizations achieve progress when they give grassroots activists a voice in the fight for their rights. Indeed, politics is a competition over whose voice prevails—not in the sense of who is loudest, but rather whose views prevail. The role of advocacy groups is to ensure that the voice of their constituents and supporters is heard in the political debate. Yet, oftentimes it is the people most affected by a policy decision who go unheard.

In order for someone to be heard, the person receiving the message must grant the other person a voice (i.e., by listening or creating a process where someone's voice is heard).[50]

Unfortunately, the patterns of behavior in Congress ensure that the voices of individuals are marginalized. For instance, individual letters to members of Congress are handled by low-level staff, as are meetings with individual constituents. Witnesses at hearings are usually the experts or heads of large organizations, not ordinary people. And of course, only members can speak on the floor of the House and Senate. Constituents are certainly important, and legislators do take them seriously. But individual constituents, acting alone, have a very limited impact on policy.

The best way to ensure that the voice of your constituents and supporters is heard and that people have an impact on policy is to organize. This is one of the key rules of the legislative process. Legislators find it easier to decide who to listen to when faced with organizations whose views, track record, and reputation are known. By organizing, you are making it more likely that your "voice" will cause a back-and-forth exchange that leads to a legislator adopting your cause, changing his or her views or, best of all, taking action on your behalf.

Legislators have chosen to grant advocacy organizations a voice. Seize that opportunity by organizing the people and giving them voice directly and through your organization.

41

The Bottom Line

1. The people who are most directly affected by the problem you are trying to solve are among your strongest advocates. Give them a voice.

2. Look for and incorporate the voices of people who may not be your most obvious allies or supporters.

3. Engage the grassroots by enabling people to contact legislators or attend a rally.

4. Give people the opportunity to be creative in their advocacy—they may surprise you and give your movement some real momentum.

5. Be ready to engage in direct action and even civil disobedience to ensure your voice is heard.

The District of Columbia's official license plates bear the movement's message:
"Taxation without Representation"

DC Voting Rights champion Representative Tom Davis introducing legislation

At a rally supporting compromise legislation, first row from left: former Secretary Jack Kemp, "shadow" DC Senator Paul Strauss, Ilir Zherka, Mayor Adrian Fenty, and "shadow" DC Senator Michael Brown

DC Vote Public Affairs Director Eugene D. Kinlow engages in community outreach with members of Youth Leadership Greater Washington

DC residents march to Capitol Building, urging action on the DC Voting Rights Act

Wearing tri-quarter hats and holding tea bags, activists stage direct-action protest outside Speaker John Boehner's home in DC

DC Delegate Eleanor Holmes Norton addresses supporters at 2011 White House Rally designed to pressure President Barack Obama to stand with DC in budget fights

DC's elected officials, led by Mayor Vincent Gray (sitting 4th from left) and Council Chair Kwame Brown (sitting 2nd from left), and activists stage civil disobedience outside US Senate

VI. Use the Outside Game to Influence Policymakers

Find ways to ensure that you link your activities to the ultimate goal: Achieving Social Change.

The Story

"Potential funders and foundations want to know, how does all of this activity— petition signing, rallies, merchandise, and public education—lead to legislative action?" asked Daniel Solomon, one of DC Vote Founders, during a planning meeting after I joined DC Vote in 2002. That was a very good question. Grassroots advocacy organizations spend a great deal of time trying to engage their members in these types of activities. When you add fundraising and administrative work, it may seem like you spend a lot of time on activities that are not directed at policymakers. With a little creativity, however, you can ensure that even seemingly unrelated activities influence legislators, their staff, and people in the executive branch.

We came up with a simple chart to show how all these activities at DC Vote are linked to each other and, ultimately, directed at the Congress.

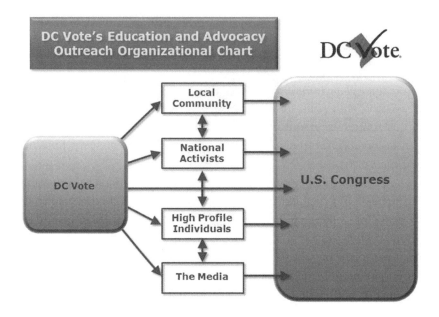

Diagram 5: DC Vote Education and Advocacy Outreach Organizational Chart

Your goal should be to direct seemingly unrelated activities toward policymakers as much as possible. Start with your "base," those people who are most affected by the problem that you are trying to solve. Your base will donate money, walk the halls of Congress, and ask their family and friends to make phone calls and write letters.

Over the years, I have found that the best tool for engaging people in the first instance is a petition. When you are at community events educating the general public about your mission or if you're advertising on the Internet, ask people to sign a petition directed at the legislative or the executive branch. You will capture the signers' contact information so you can engage them in the future, while directing their energy immediately toward policymakers. Petition drives are particularly useful to organizations that are primarily focused on education, because you are not lobbying (as defined by the IRS[51]) when you ask people to sign a petition calling on elected officials simply to fix a problem (e.g., provide voting rights, end hunger, etc.), and you do not mention a specific bill. If you are not concerned about racking up lobbying hours, your organization can request that people sign a letter to Congress in support of or in opposition to legislation. This is an even more direct way of both capturing information and directly influencing policymakers.

People also love merchandise. At DC Vote, we created T-shirts and bumper stickers that are widely used in the city. When people attach bumper stickers to their cars or wear T-shirts around town, they help to influence two other groups that are critical to your campaign: the media and potential champions, because these folks are affected by a buzz surrounding an issue or campaign. So, by distributing merchandise, you can also have a policy impact.

Additionally, generate news stories with your activities because legislators and their staff pay attention to the media. In February 2009, pro-gun Democrats attached an amendment to the DC Voting Rights Act that would eliminate DC's gun laws. This amendment caused DC Vote a great deal of hardship in the House, where over sixty Democrats voted to support the amendment the year before. As the House grappled with what to do, one Democratic leader made the case that DC might be willing to take the amendment, or support a compromise version in order to secure voting representation. To make his case, he cited an article by Marc Fisher in the Washington Post, where Fisher made that very point.[52] Clearly, he learned very important information from the article and used that information to push for moving the bill with the gun amendment.

The best way to generate news is to have your base demonstrate intensity by engaging in newsworthy activities such as rallies, demonstrations, and lobby days. DC Vote routinely came up with ways to make news despite the absence of significant legislative progress in Congress. We generated nearly 4,000 news stories on DC voting rights during a ten-year period. For example, in 2002, media outlets nationwide carried stories about DC residents who were burning their tax forms on April 15th ("Tax Day"), as a way of illustrating the "No Taxation without Representation" slogan. On July Fourth of that year, a group of residents presented a Declaration of Reunification with Great Britain to the British embassy in Washington. Ultimately, these events were designed to create a buzz and momentum in Congress by attracting media coverage in America and around the world.

Make sure to forward news stories to legislators and their staff. They understand that thousands, if not millions, of people are reading these stories. With news coverage, your issue automatically becomes relevant. Other powerful people who could be champions for your cause will also start to be influenced by media stories that cover grassroots activity.

For example, when Hurricane Katrina hit the Gulf Coast, Jack Kemp sprang into action. I heard him on radio and television talking about how Republicans need to refocus on urban areas and urban problems. For many years, Kemp was a powerful voice within the Republican Party in favor of civil rights and urban renewal policies.[53] I had been in conversations with his son, Jimmy, for a couple of years trying to recruit him and his father to our cause. The more we were in the news, the greater their interest.

Because Kemp was trying to get the Republicans to focus on urban areas and minorities after Hurricane Katrina, we now had an opening. I called Jimmy and suggested that Kemp author an article calling the District of Columbia "Ground Zero" in the Republican effort to champion urban renewal and civil rights. They agreed to do it. When the article was published in late September 2005, we distributed it widely on Capitol Hill.[54] Kemp helped us elevate our profile because people saw that someone of his stature believed in our mission. Thus, people's perception of DC Vote changed, and we were taken more seriously. Kemp also attracted media attention, which in turn helped us energize our base of supporters, resulting in even more pressure on Congress.

Additional Stories

Advocates agree that grassroots activities have to be carefully tailored. Some legislators respond more than others to activities held in their home districts. Some activities are also more effective in election years than in other years. Considering the demographic of the activist is also important, says Tanya Clay House, the former Director of Public Policy of People For the American Way. For example, certain issues lend themselves more to waging online campaigns if the age groups that are most involved are tech-savvy. Other issues may involve constituencies that are more easily organized for demonstrations and marches.

Sometimes communications with legislators are most effective when they take place far from their legislative chambers. Sarah Dufendach, Vice President for Legislative Affairs at Common Cause, notes that generating constituent visitors to the local district offices can get more attention because there is less competition for media coverage. Common Cause's Pennsylvania activists met with their delegates at the local district office during an election year and persuaded them to pledge support for public financing of elections.

Timing is also crucial, notes Josh Horwitz, executive director of the Coalition to Stop Gun Violence. Sometimes, planning actions to coincide with busy periods is the best tactic if you are playing defense and opposing a bill. Members of Congress have tight schedules and often feel pressure to return to their districts or spend time on the campaign trail. If grassroots activities are timed to provoke doubt or demonstrate opposition as legislative time is running out, votes can be made to appear too controversial or complicated, and thus successfully delayed or derailed.

One senior aide to a member of the Democratic leadership cautions that advocacy groups should keep their activities carefully focused. In all communications, advocates should focus on the direct impact their issue has on the legislator's district. Flooding a legislator's office line with telephone calls is unnecessary, according to this staffer, and receiving repeated calls from voters outside the district may actually have a negative impact. He notes that constituent calls always make an impact, so there is no need for a flood of calls. Likewise, he says, a flood of e-mails from an advocacy campaign are not persuasive; they "look contrived," and just end up "in e-mail heaven."

MoveOn and others pioneered technology that allows people to easily send thousands of e-mails to a legislator. Because this process has become so easy, there is an assumption among many staffers that constituents are not as personally invested in the argument they are presenting. A more personalized letter is certainly more persuasive. Nonetheless, mass communications can have an impact. So, use whatever tactics fit at the moment.

Lobby days are the most effective in directing the outside message in. Whether at the Hill office or in the home district, these communications are most effective when constituents are involved in person. While this senior staffer concedes that public rallies do help get press attention, which is very important, such demonstrations are "just the beginning" and must be large, diverse, or dramatic enough to warrant serious attention from a legislator.

The Tools: The Butterfly Effect

Some advocates make the mistake of thinking that their actions—the "exchanges" as defined by HSD— will automatically draw the attention of legislators. The assumption here is that because people are speaking or are active, folks on the

Hill will go out of their way to find out what's happening. But we know that there are distinct patterns of behavior within the legislature. Those patterns are dominated by: committee hearings and markups; votes on the floor; events sponsored by the legislator (like press conferences); interactions with colleagues; fundraising activities; and meetings with outside groups (lobbyists, government agencies, advocacy groups, and constituents). Moreover, legislators often focus on the news that impacts their district or state.

A smart advocate, therefore, will understand that these patterns exist in the lives of legislators and that you have to work really hard to get a legislator's attention, and even harder to get them to agree with you or do something for you.

Much of what we do as public interest advocates is to "flap our wings" like a butterfly through a wide range of activities in the hope that we spark a chain reaction that could end up having a profound impact on the political system.

In HSD, this phenomenon is called the "butterfly effect." The idea is that small changes or actions over time cause major shifts in systems. We have all experienced or witnessed this effect before. A friend or a colleague makes an off-handed remark (a compliment or an insult) that shifts your relationship with that person. Or a governor engages in an affair that results in his resignation and a shift in power to the other party. These occurrences are just like butterflies that flap their wings in the Pacific Rim and cause hurricanes thousands of miles away in the Caribbean.[55]

While not all of your activities can directly involve legislators or their staff, it is imperative that most of your activities in some way loop back into the everyday patterns of the legislative cycle. The best way to achieve that goal is to create media stories in outlets that cater to the legislators you are trying to impact (e.g., publications and websites that are political or are in a legislator's district or state), even when you're not directly lobbying the legislature. Additionally, establish relationships with legislative and administration staffers. Add them to your database. Send them periodic updates of your activities or news clips and website links to stories about your issue. But be careful not to overwhelm them, otherwise they will tune you and your issue out.

Let's think back to the Landscape Diagram in the Introduction. Your goal is to achieve agreement about your issue among legislators and their staff, to create a commitment to a specific legislative remedy, and to secure actual movement of a bill. The activities associated with the outside game should all be designed to move your issue through a series of exchanges and a softening of differences, down the diagram from the self-organizing zone to the organized zone. The best way to achieve that goal is to direct your outside game toward legislators, their staff, the executive branch, and other policy makers.

As Glenda Eoyang, founder of HSD, puts it, "Every little thing that happens might turn out to be a major influence on the future of the world. We cannot tell which factors will represent butterfly effects and which ones will cause only predictable changes. That is the nature of a complex, chaotic system."[56] A good example of this effect is the suggestion Congressman Tom Davis made on a radio show that Congress should pass a bill creating a seat for DC and one for Utah (see Chapter IV). That off-handed remark changed the patterns of the DC Democracy Movement, leading to six years of work by thousands of people spending millions of dollars to enact such a bill.

Make sure you flap your wings in the direction of decision makers— the closer you get the better.

The Bottom Line

1. Winning the inside game starts with recruiting outside supporters.

2. Engage in activity outside the halls of the legislative and executive branch that generates news stories because they impact perceptions among the inside players.

3. Create a cycle where "outside game" activities result in media stories, which result in more legislative attention, which feeds your recruitment of people for grassroots activities.

4. Ultimately, most of your activities should aim to increase your presence and influence among decision makers.

VII. Communicate at All Times in All Directions

Use websites, e-mail, social networks, and newsletters to communicate with everyone, but don't forget that talking to people directly is still most effective

The Story

I was in a casual conversation with a board member who expressed surprise that DC Vote had decided to embrace a specific piece of legislation, a decision that had occurred a couple of years earlier. Walking away from that conversation I thought, "How could this person be so in the dark? We send e-mail updates, monthly news bulletins, newsletters, and so forth. We also put all our statements and activities on our website!" But there are so many people close to DC Vote who are in the dark about something: the DC Council member who urges us to develop a curriculum for public school classes and to teach kids about the issue, when we have been doing both of those things for years; the reporter who writes a feature length story on DC voting rights focusing on the reasons why the issue is hot again, but does not mention the plethora of activities DC Vote has initiated to draw attention to the issue and to move legislation; or the DC Vote staffer who works in an office with fewer than ten people, but is not aware we are planning a Veterans' Day Rally that would take place within two weeks.

57

In this "Communications Age," we are totally overwhelmed by information. Consequently, our attention span is shorter, and it is harder to get us to absorb and retain information. According to a publication by the Union for Concerned Scientists, the average American is exposed to about three thousand advertising messages each day.[57] The result: organizations have to communicate in all directions at all times. You cannot assume that your message is getting through to the right people, or that they understand it.

The best way to reach people, however, is to talk to them directly. Of course, this is very time-consuming. Therefore, ask yourself, "Who are the people that I need to reach on a regular basis?" For me, this list includes concentric circles of people that ripple out in order of importance: my staff, my board, key legislative and government staff, key reporters, coalition partners, major donors, and key volunteers, as shown in Diagram 4 below. We work really hard every week to speak directly with as many people on this list as possible: regular meetings, phone calls, conversations at events, short e-mails, lunch meetings, and briefings. We routinely use each of these tools to keep people updated about our activities and the status of our legislation.

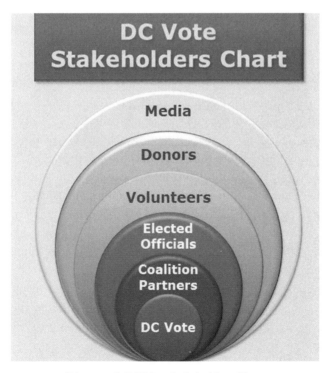

Diagram 6: DC Vote Stakeholders Chart

58

People who are "connectors" engage personally and directly with your core supporters more effectively than other people. It is in their DNA. In Malcolm Gladwell's bestseller *The Tipping Point*, he identified "connectors" as those who "are the kinds of people who know everyone" and who have "a special gift for bringing the world together" and "who link us up with the world."[58] This "handful of people with a truly extraordinary knack of making friends and acquaintances" make a huge difference, in part because "they manage to occupy many different worlds and subcultures and niches."[59] For advocacy organizations, employ people who are connectors: they are critical to your success. Find them. Hire them. Keep them happy. They are gold.

At DC Vote, Eugene Dewitt Kinlow serves as a classic connector, with that "combination of curiosity, self-confidence, sociability, and energy" that Gladwell describes.[60] Without any prompting from me, Eugene would attend, in just one week, several evening meetings hosted by groups like the DC Democratic State Committee, the Gertrude Stein Club, DC for Democracy, the DC NAACP, and many others. On Monday mornings, he would be aglow if he attended at least three community events during the weekend. The result: Eugene would produce volunteers whenever we needed them and helped us raise significant funds every year. He also has strong relationships with DC Council members, advisors in the DC Mayor's office, and Hill staffers. As Gladwell concludes, "The point about connectors is that, by having a foot in so many different worlds, they have the effect of bringing them all together."[61]

Eugene is a natural networking machine. The rest of us have to work at it. Your campaign's success significantly depends on the relationships you have with others, especially the people in power who can help you. Talk to those folks frequently. As Gladwell notes, "Word of mouth is— even in this age of mass communications and multimillion-dollar advertising campaigns— still the most important form of human communication."[62]

The Obama Campaign of 2008 understood this lesson well. Although many observers cited the campaign's revolutionary use of the Internet as a main reason for the campaign's success, David Plouffe credited his field operation as their strongest asset: "'There's nothing more valuable than a human being talking to a human being. Nothing.'"[63]

Talking to legislators directly is critical. Most lobbyists spend a great deal of money to attend political and organizational fundraisers so that they can have access to legislators. These events are political goldmines. It can take you months before you get a meeting with a legislator (who often will cancel and send a staff person to meet with you instead). But you can reach multiple legislators in just one night without scheduling an appointment in advance. For instance, in early 2009, I attended a fundraiser for the Alzheimer's Association, held at the National Building Museum. Philanthropist and DC Vote Board member Trish Vradenburg invited me, thinking it would be useful for me to make some connections for DC Vote. Within twenty minutes, I thanked Senator Frank Lautenberg (D-NJ) for his support, received advice from former Speaker Newt Gingrich, talked strategy with Majority Leader Steny Hoyer (D-MD), and had an honest discussion about our chances in the Senate with freshman Senator Mark Warner (D-VA). All of those discussions took place during the VIP reception. This is just one example of why it is critical to recruit people who have the means to secure this kind of access for you. If not, spend your money wisely on gaining that access.

One way to do that is by establishing a Political Action Committee (a "PAC"). PACs can make direct contributions to political campaigns, as well as provide support or opposition to a candidate. By creating a PAC and raising a meaningful amount of money for it, you can get significant assess to legislators. The private sector plays this game exceedingly well. Nearly 1,600 corporations have a PAC. Collectively, they give millions of dollars in campaign contributions to political candidates. In 2009 alone, the Federal Elections Commission noted that "corporate PACs reported making $72.1 million in contributions to candidates."[64] There are some legal limitations about which you must be aware. For instance, charitable 501 (c) (3) organizations cannot be affiliated with a PAC, but 501 (c) (4) organizations can be. If you can raise enough money, creating and using a PAC to gain access to legislators is very helpful.

The Marijuana Policy Project established a PAC for this very reason. "When you're a midsized nonprofit organization like MPP is, you can sometimes get ten minutes of a congressperson's time in their office, but your meeting can easily get bumped," says Rob Kampia, Executive Director of MPP in D.C. "But if the nonprofit also has a PAC, then a $500 or $1,000 donation at a congressperson's campaign fundraising reception on Capitol Hill guarantees you access to the congressperson, his or her staff, and the congressperson's colleagues who also show up to the fundraising reception to show support for their colleague's reelection campaign."

Although viewed by some in the mainstream as a marginal group, by maximizing access to decision-makers, MPP has been instrumental in enacting medical marijuana laws in the District of Columbia, Hawaii, Maine, Michigan, Montana, Rhode Island, and Vermont, and assisted in enacting laws in the other eight states that have medical marijuana laws. Also, MPP decriminalized the possession of marijuana for all uses in Massachusetts—the first such statewide ballot initiative to pass.

The best way to reach your donors, volunteers, and general supporters is to maximize all of the modern communications methods: a website, newsletters, annual reports, e-mail updates, and social networking sites. Of course, most nonprofits have limited resources. So, you may need to pick and choose where you focus your communications efforts. At the top of your list should be a very well-organized, frequently updated website. As we discuss in the next chapter, legislative staff are highly dependent on you to provide short and concise information. Usually, they will ask you to e-mail it to them. They also need to find documents on your website quickly and easily. The same is true for the media, scholars, and potential donors.

I have also found that paper newsletters are still very effective ways to communicate. People who came of age before the Internet will often skip over e-mails from your organization. I asked Tom Sherwood, a reporter for *NBC News*, whether he read our monthly e-mail bulletins or the newsletters. He said something I hear from many others as well: he always skips our e-mail bulletins, but reads the newsletter from cover to cover. Other people (like my wife, who is a busy communications lawyer), however, will glance at short e-mails, but don't have the time to read an entire newsletter. The point is to diversify your message delivery system so that your message reaches as many people as possible.

Additional Stories

Nancy Zirkin, executive vice president of The Leadership Conference on Civil and Human Rights, says organizations need to employ the "whole package" at all levels and maintain a stream of communication coming from a diverse mix of people and voices at the grassroots, grasstops, and official levels. This variety and consistency becomes even more important if the issue is a controversial one.

Noah Winer, formerly with MoveOn, described the "highest order of advocacy" as an in-person meeting with media representatives, held outside the offices of members of Congress, and conducted by credible spokespeople. This one event allows an organization to reach two audiences— a legislator and the general public— while also providing opportunities for volunteer activism. Winer cites MoveOn's efforts in 2009 to promote clean energy job creation as an example. To publicize their position in favor of federal funding for clean energy jobs, MoveOn organized a Clean Energy Jobs Day. Business owners and others who work in those industries held educational press conferences outside legislative offices, showing photos or offering reporters tours of their workplaces. Winer notes that involving these businesspeople in sharing their experiences in person increased the campaign's impact.

A senior legislative staffer in the House emphasizes that "without continuous follow-up, launching a nonprofit advocacy effort is a waste of time." He says, "The role of nonprofits is essential" to keep issues alive and prominent in the public debate. By maintaining a constant stream of accurate information, "by nudging, calling, visiting," and by motivating the grassroots in the states and legislative districts to continue to support their position, "nonprofits make a huge impact on the legislative process."

The Tools: Crossing Boundaries

Under HSD, a boundary "is the area that lies between two different parts of a system."[65] Boundaries are plentiful in the complex system of Congress. Personal offices, committee staff, Democrat, Republican, House, Senate, advocates, lobbyists, executive branch, government agencies— these all represent boundaries within the system. Every nonprofit has its shares of boundaries too: individual staff, work teams, departments, board members, volunteers, legislators, coalition partners, gender, ethnicity, culture, etc. Boundaries are another way to describe "containers." Momentum occurs and the possibility of change exists when these boundaries meet and the differences force an exchange of views, information, and perspective.

In nature and human behavior, interaction at the boundaries can be difficult or intense. This is especially true when boundaries are clear and distinct, such as between an advocacy organization and a legislator. Consequently, lots of people actively try to avoid crossing boundaries. E-mail, voice-mail, and postings on social media sites allow people to avoid interacting directly with others, while giving them the feeling that they are communicating. These tools have their place and are effective when used in concert with direct face-to-face interaction across boundaries.

As an advocate, resist giving in to fears about boundaries. For example, don't assume that someone who has a certain party or group affiliation will be either for or against you. At DC Vote, we approach all organizations, both parties, and folks in the DC government as potential allies. We refuse to let boundaries between us and other people create barriers to collaboration.

Try to bring people who represent different boundaries together often. You can do that by creating or joining coalitions. Organize in-person meetings where you bring together legislative staff, coalition partners, your staff, board member, donors, and others. All of the different roles and opinions presented will better inform and strengthen the tactics you employ to achieve your goals.

When you discover that a boundary is causing you problems, you can take a few steps outlined by Glenda Eoyang: [66]

- Convene a group to brainstorm which boundaries are causing a problem
- From the list, select the one boundary that seems to be the most important
- Describe in detail the apparent differences across the boundaries
- Identify how the character of the boundary needs to change
- Brainstorm for tactics that will change the nature of the boundary
- Select one tactic and try that first
- Keep adjusting tactics as needed

Above all else, cross boundaries regularly and in-person. You will communicate much more effectively, which, in turn, will significantly increase the possibility that you will achieve your goals.

The Bottom Line

1. Organizations have to communicate in all directions at all times.

2. You cannot assume that your message is getting through to the right people or that they understand it.

3. The most effective way to communicate with people is by talking to them directly.

4. Utilize all the modern tools of communication; make sure you create and maintain a comprehensive website.

5. Refuse to make assumptions about boundaries between you and others

6. Where possible, cross boundaries often.

VIII. Work the Inside Game

Advocacy organizations must use their board members, donors, lobbyists, and others to directly engage legislators and their staff.

The Story

"Rallies, protests, maybe even some civil disobedience, those are things I could put on TV," said a reporter. "Meetings on the Hill with members of Congress and their staff, those aren't stories that I can cover." A group of us from DC Vote went to visit the reporter in 2005. Our goal was to explain all the work we had been doing on the Hill to get people interested in the DC Voting Rights Act. The reporter, on the other hand, was expressing the view of many in the industry: nitty-gritty meetings on Capitol Hill are not newsworthy events.

Mass rallies and protests definitely are critical to winning. But there is no substitute for engaging legislators and their staff or people in the executive branch as directly and as often as possible. A legislative staffer put it this way during an interview:

> "The most important thing an advocacy organization can do is develop a trusting relationship with a member of Congress, Senator, and their staff. What we need more than anything else is information. We need organizations that are experts on the details and can provide clear and concise information on a moment's notice. We need organizations that

are honest brokers, ones that can provide detailed information on factual questions even if that information doesn't help their cause. The second most important thing is for organizations to have one-on-one meetings, and on occasion, group briefings for legislative staff. Those are the two things that are most impactful."

The private sector understands very well the primacy of working the inside game. The Center for Responsive Politics reports that over $3.49 billion was spent in 2009 on lobbying Congress and federal agencies. Within that group, Exxon Mobil spent $27 million, General Electric spent well over $25 million, while Fed-Ex spent $16 million and AT&T Inc. spent $14 million on lobbying expenses.[67]

As we were developing bipartisan support in the House for the DC Voting Rights Act, we turned to one of our champions, former Secretary Jack Kemp. Kemp provided us with a credible Republican voice in the media. Kemp also helped us to work the inside game. In 2007, we were in search of an additional conservative Republican ally in Congress. Our bill was moving through the oversight and judiciary committees. We sat down with Jimmy Kemp (Jack's son) and JT Taylor (the head of Jack's firm) to review the list of members on the committees. Representative Mike Pence, a Republican from Indiana, was one among a number of potential champions Jimmy and JT identified for Kemp to contact. We had absolutely no ties to Pence. Our coalition partners had very few members in Indiana. None of our partners had worked with Pence before. For all of those reasons, Pence was the perfect "unusual suspect." But, we could not reach Pence, let alone convince him to take up our cause, without an inside connection.

That connection was Jack Kemp. Kemp called Pence and talked with him a few times before the judiciary committee markup on March 14, 2007.[68] The conversations Kemp had with Pence about the bill were standard fare: Kemp stressed the overall importance of DC voting rights and the leadership that Republicans ought to take on civil rights issues. We could have made exactly the same points to Pence. So, it wasn't the message that got through. It was the messenger.

Pence trusted and admired Kemp, and so he was willing to listen to him because he believed that Kemp had his best interests in mind.

Pence also considered supporting us because Ken Starr had testified that our bill was constitutional. Tom Davis had recruited Starr in 2004 to research the constitutionality of the bill and to testify in support of it, both of which he did. Starr was the lead prosecutor during the impeachment of President Bill Clinton. Consequently, he had credibility among Republicans. Pence saw him as a credible source of information on the constitutionality question.

Pence had not yet committed to supporting us as late as the morning of the markup. I woke up that morning believing that Kemp should try Pence again, which he did. As I sat in the committee room of the Rayburn House Office Building, I received an e-mail on my Blackberry from JT saying that Pence was leaning our way, but wanted to review the Starr testimony again. Terrance Norflis, a Norton staffer, went to his office where he downloaded and printed out the testimony from our website. Within ten minutes of the e-mail from JT, Pence had the testimony in front of him, which he read before voting "yes" in support of our bill. Pence then became a vocal supporter, speaking on the floor of the House during the debate on the bill and also authoring an op-ed article on the Human Events' website.[69]

The DC Voting Rights Act passed the House on April 19, 2007, because a large number of people worked both the inside and the outside game.[70] Del. Norton worked with Chairmen Henry Waxman (D-CA) and John Conyers (D-MI) to get the bill before their respective committees. She also worked with Speaker Nancy Pelosi and Majority Leader Steny Hoyer to schedule time on the House floor. Nancy Zirkin, executive vice president of the Leadership Conference on Civil and Human Rights, talked to senior staff on those committees, and met with Hoyer and with Pelosi's senior staff. Congressman Davis worked the Republicans on his committee and other moderates, helping to convince twenty-two Republicans to vote in favor of the bill. Kemp got Representative Dan Burton to switch his vote from "no" to "yes" by talking to him in one of the back rooms during the markup. Carl Thorsen, a Republican lobbyist, gathered intelligence from a number of our Republican targets. We replicated this approach in the Senate. Senator Orrin Hatch (R-UT) reached out to his colleagues and helped secure the support of seven other Republicans. Also, Kathy Kemper and George Vradenburg (both active politically with personal ties to legislators) talked directly to at least six different senators, helping to secure the votes of a few of them.

DC Vote's role was to supplement and coordinate all of the inside activity, while also providing information to committee staff, finding witnesses for the hearings, and providing briefings and information to staff. DC Vote was a credible source of information and could exert leadership among all these elected officials because we represented people in the city and had assembled a coalition of organizations which, in turn, represented millions of people around the country. The rallies, constituent calls to Congress, citizen-lobby visits, advertisements, etc., were all critical to creating pressure for action on the DC VRA. Ultimately, however, we had to bring together politicians, lobbyists, and campaign donors to work the inside game, and use their existing relationships to talk directly with representatives and senators and persuade them to support us. Those interactions were the key factors that made a difference during our fight, which led to 242 votes in the House and fifty-seven votes in the Senate in support of the DC Voting Rights Act. Although that was not enough to overcome a filibuster that year, we received more support for our cause than at any time in the previous thirty years.

Additional Stories

In a *New York Times* article, columnist Frank Rich explores how private companies used lobbyists during the 2009 fight on health care reform and used campaign donations to get access to legislative leaders.[71] He describes how private companies with an interest in the outcome hired former members of Congress to help them influence the debate. Rich points out that "UnitedHealth's hired Beltway gunslingers include both Elmendorf Strategies and [Tom] Daschle," a former key House staffer and former Senate majority leader, respectively. In addition, he notes that "the company's in-house lobbyist is a former chief of staff to Steny Hoyer, the House Majority Leader. Dick Gephardt consults there too." Dick Gephardt is another former House member who served as House majority leader from 1989 to 1995 and as minority leader from 1995 to 2003. Rich also details UnitedHealth's activities on the other side of the aisle. GOP leaders who rejected a public health care option often cite health care research data by the Lewin Group, which was "actually bought by a subsidiary of UnitedHealth in 2007." Rich observes that Republican representatives "John Boehner and Eric Cantor—who use Lewin's findings to scare voters about a 'government takeover' of health care—are big recipients of UnitedHealth campaign cash." The example of UnitedHealth demonstrates how private sector organizations enlist influential leaders to help them play the inside game.

Wade Henderson, president and CEO of the Leadership Conference on Civil and Human Rights, thinks the inside game is "critically important." He ought to know. With over 200 organizations joined together, Wade runs one of the largest, most successful advocacy coalitions in America. He has been a central player in many inside game strategies over the course of three decades. In fact, Wade spends most of his "advocacy" time talking directly with legislators and their staff, not organizing grassroots activity. Here is Wade's take on the inside game:

"The inside game is as important as the typical grassroots and grasstops outside game. It may be less visible and certainly less understood. But, successful organizations cultivate direct relationships with legislators and their staff over many years. We run with the foxes and the hounds – both our natural allies and our at-times opponents. Very often, access is tied to money. Groups and individuals who can give campaign donations have direct access to elected officials. We have access to these officials because of our over-arching mission, the millions of Americans who make up the membership of The Leadership Conference's more than 200 organizations, and the aggressive outreach efforts of our senior staff and our members. The goal of nonprofits is to use that access to advance the public interest. An advocate's role must be to influence the elected officials who are taking part in cutting the legislative deals."

Wade counsels that sometimes you have to combine the outside and inside game even to get your friends to "do the right thing." During the 2009 health care reform effort, Wade was displeased that the bills making their way through a Democratic Congress did not have antidiscrimination provisions in them. The Leadership Conference ran ads highlighting the bill's flaws in communities of color in swing states: Arkansas, Florida, Louisiana, and North Carolina. All of these states were carried by Barack Obama in 2008 and/or in some instances represented by moderate Democrats who would care what civil rights constituents in these communities thought of the bill. The Leadership Conference's goal was to get the attention of the White House. They achieved their goal. Soon after the ads starting running, senior White House officials held conference calls with the media and others to explain the president's position. After achieving their first goal through the outside game, the Leadership Conference worked the inside game. They met with senior staff at the White House to advocate for their position and to warn that they would keep "connecting voters to policy makers" if antidiscrimination language was not added to the health care bill.

President Barack Obama signed the Patient Protection and Affordable Care Act into law on March 23, 2010. Using a combination of the outside and inside game, The Leadership Conference secured the inclusion of Section 1557 in the act. That section prohibits insurers from discriminating based on race, gender, and disability. It also provides for a private right of action. This was clearly a major achievement for the civil rights community.

The Tools: Understanding and Using the Feedback Loop

Everyone has heard the term "feedback" and understands that it is information you receive in reaction to something you did or said. However, that definition is static and not reflective of the real world. Feedback does not simply end when it comes back to you. In fact, you absorb that information and act on it in some way. This process, under human systems dynamics, is known as the transforming feedback loop:

A transforming feedback loop is the form of communication that passes across the boundary between any two parts of a complex system. One part of the system changes and the change is transmitted to another part of the system. The second part responds to the change in the first, and its change is transmitted back to the first, which responds with a change of its own. [72]

For best results, the loop must be established and continued in person: "Human contact remains the richest context for transforming communications."[73] This type of back and forth in-person is the fuel of the legislative process. Legislators talk to each other all the time. In fact, the feedback loop is the main way work gets done in Congress. Staffers are constantly reminding their bosses to find so-and-so on the "floor" to discuss some legislation. For most pieces of legislation that are enacted into law, this exchange occurs between legislators of the majority party. Private sector companies understand this very well. They employ thousands of lobbyists to create transforming-feedback loops between themselves and members of Congress. In fact, the word lobbying derives from the activity of advocates spending time in the lobbies just to create opportunities for face-to-face communication with legislators.

To be effective, public interest advocates need to do the same thing by working the inside game. Here are some tips. For communication to be transforming (*i.e.* result in change), it has to be in context. You can't just tell legislators to support your bill. You have to explain why your bill is important to you and, preferably, their constituents. Visit as many legislative offices as possible to explain your position. You also have to be open to the feedback you receive and be willing to adapt when you hear the same things from legislators who support your position or when opponents demonstrate the power to stop you. Balance the negative with the positive feedback you give to legislators and their staff. Don't be shrill all the time. Even your supporters will grow weary of you. Be cautious. Not all feedback is transformational. Some legislator's reactions may not gain much traction and not all concerns with your bill need to be addressed. Work all the levers by visiting multiple legislators and their staff. Never expect that one relationship or one conversation will create the momentum you need to succeed. Follow up. A solitary contact without follow-up is the equivalent of feedback that comes to an end without creating a reaction (*i.e.*, a loop). Your bill will go nowhere if you do not follow up, in person and often, with legislators and their staff.

The Bottom Line

1. Place a premium on direct interaction with legislators and their staff.

2. Ensure you can provide quality information on a moment's notice.

3. Be honest and straightforward with your legislative allies.

4. Build credibility by resisting the temptation to exaggerate or stretch the facts.

5. Create and participate in face-to-face transforming feedback loops.

6. Follow up!

IX. Elections Matter

You can become a more effective advocate if your organization works to promote and defeat candidates.

The Story

President Barack Obama had a laundry list of important items he wanted the US Congress to take up in 2009: rescuing the American economy; reforming health care; transforming our energy policy; and overhauling our foreign policy. Our goal was a tad less ambitious— to get Congress to consider the DC Voting Rights Act within the first one hundred days. Imagine our delight when Senate Majority Leader Harry Reid announced in early February that the Senate would take action on the bill. House Majority Leader Steny Hoyer followed suit, announcing that the full House would take up the bill in early March. At that moment, it looked like our dreams had come true— the bill had leap-frogged over hundreds of other pieces of legislation and was on a glide path to victory!

The 2008 election mattered a great deal to the DC Voting Rights Movement. Democrats, almost-certain to vote for the DC VRA, picked up eight seats in the Senate, which meant we had enough votes to prevent a filibuster. Democrats picked up twenty-one seats in the House, padding our formidable vote margin from 2007. And Barack Obama was elected president. He was a cosponsor of the bill in the preceding Congress and would certainly sign it into law. People were so convinced we were on the verge of winning that I began getting calls and e-mails from people asking me about the victory party after our bill was signed into law, and whether we could get them into the signing ceremony at the White House.

I spent the first few months after the election telling people that our opponents were both smart and determined to stop us, therefore, we should be cautiously optimistic. So I was more angry than surprised when Senator Reid's staff told us just two days before the vote that he would support an amendment to the DC VRA that would gut the District's gun laws. It became very clear that we would lose the vote on the gun amendment because, while Democrats picked up seats in Congress, many of those additional Democrats were in favor of gun rights and beholden to, or fearful of, the National Rifle Association (NRA).

The Senate adopted the gun amendment by an overwhelming vote of 62-36, with twenty-two Democrats voting for the bill. The sponsor, Republican Senator John Ensign, intended the amendment to be a "poison pill" (*i.e.*, legislative language added to the underlying bill, making it unacceptable to its supporters)[74]. After the bill passed the Senate, the House Democratic leadership determined that they could not bring the DC VRA up for a vote unless they also allowed a vote on the gun amendment. Ensign's strategy was successful. DC's elected leaders and a number of our coalition partners, and ultimately DC Vote as well, were unwilling to support movement of the DC VRA in the House because of the prospect of the gun amendment becoming law. Ensign, the NRA, and others effectively blocked the DC VRA from being enacted, even though we had a strong majority of the Congress ready to vote for the non-amended version.

The Senators and Representatives who supported the gun amendment understood that elections matter, as does the NRA.

The NRA won this fight because they work vigorously to promote and defeat candidates for office. The NRA has been active in legislative affairs since 1934 and formed the NRA Institute for Legislative Action in 1975 to organize political "defense" of the Second Amendment. The NRA Foundation was created in 1990 to raise millions of dollars to fund "gun safety and educational projects" designed to influence the public debate about gun ownership in America. The organization is structured to leverage local activists, lobbyists, and policy research to achieve NRA objectives. As former Clinton spokesman George Stephanopoulos said about the NRA, "They call their congressmen. They write. They vote. They contribute. And they get what they want over time." These days, "they" number more than eighty staff and millions of members—a number that, according to the NRA, has more than tripled since 1978.[75]

In the 2008 elections, as in many previous elections, the gun lobby donated money to candidates; they rated candidates on gun rights issues and widely distributed the results; and they paid for political ads. DC Vote did none of these things. While we understood the first eight strategies of advocacy outlined in this handbook, as a 501 (c)(3) educational organization in partnership with a bunch of lobbying organizations, we could not, under federal tax law, raise and spend money to influence elections.[76] Chances are your organization cannot do so either. Educational organizations can, however, engage in voter education and registration efforts, candidate forums, issue guides, and even work to get out the vote, as long as that activity is nonpartisan.

Most nonprofits do not engage in electoral politics. But know this: one of the most effective ways to pursue your agenda is through the ballot box. In fact, the District of Columbia finally achieved home rule, at the end of 1973, only after the election of 1972 helped to change the political dynamics in Congress. Most notably, longtime segregationist Representative John L. McMillan (D-SC), who served as the chairman of the House District Committee first in the mid-1940s and then continuously from 1955 through 1972, was defeated in South Carolina's Democratic primary in September 1972. McMillan was a strong opponent of democracy for the District and his committee was referred to as a "notorious graveyard for home rule" in a 1970 *Washington Post* editorial.[77] DC activists, led by Delegate Walter Fauntroy, helped defeat McMillan by traveling to South Carolina to campaign against him in his legislative district during the 1970 and 1972 election. After his defeat, the composition of the house district committee changed dramatically, making possible the enactment of home rule.[78]

Whether you win or lose a public policy fight may very well hinge on an election. Therefore, if you want to have all the advocacy tools at your disposal, you should consider creating a political organization that can engage freely in promoting and defeating candidates for office.

Additional Stories

An experienced Hill staffer observed, "Politicians are all about getting reelected." Another legislative leader commented that "some advocacy groups hide under the 501(c)3 status" and "do a disservice to their members and cause" by wholly avoiding activity during election season. He urged leaders of nonprofits and their boards to get involved as "private citizens" and "join election battles if they want to promote their legislation," and emphasized that nonprofits should hold issue forums and other nonpartisan election activities in order to "show the strength of the group and its mission" and gain "tremendous access." Remember, c (3) organizations can engage in nonpartisan election activity. You should do that as much as possible.

Elections put into motion very predictable behavioral patterns. Candidates must seek out and raise money from donors. They will contact organizations, attend their meetings, and seek their endorsements. They will create campaign events or visit public sites. Candidates might hold town hall meetings. They will likely debate their opponents, answer questions by the media, and fill out organizational questionnaires. Advocates can use all of these activities to raise questions directly to a candidate and influence the views of likely voters.

Successful advocates will be able to convey to the candidate how a cause either helps their election bid or does not hurt it. Advocacy groups can effectively demonstrate their power among a candidate's electorates by bringing local constituents to Washington, DC, getting people to vote, affecting the press in home districts, and publicizing surveys and ratings about candidates' views ahead of elections.

The leaders of MoveOn understood that 2008 would be a pivotal election for their progressive agenda. They engaged in aggressive recruiting, fundraising, and organizing strategies. MoveOn bundles donations from members, recruits volunteers, conducts phone banks, and places ads in key districts and races. These activities are intended to demonstrate the clout of progressive voters and influence elected officials' stance on the issues.

In 2008, the organization's members participated in election activities in unprecedented numbers. In the presidential race, MoveOn facilitated participation by 933,800 volunteers who logged over 20,841,507 hours and donated over $88 million for Barack Obama. In the Senate, MoveOn spent nearly $4 million for ads and direct mail in key Senate states, and supported successful challengers including Jeff Merkley in Oregon, Jeanne Shaheen in New Hampshire, and Mark Udall in Colorado. In traditionally conservative North Carolina, MoveOn raised and spent over $3 million to run ads supporting challenger Kay Hagan for the Senate. They also registered new voters in NC. Close to 44,000 new and young voters were added to the state's rolls. Obama won North Carolina's electoral votes, which went "blue" (i.e., supported the Democratic candidate) for the first time since 1976, and the Democratic candidates for governor, senator, and congressman prevailed as well. In the House, MoveOn members contributed $1 million to help put Democratic candidates over the top.[79]

One of MoveOn's key activities is an innovative approach to phone banking. MoveOn pioneered web technology to make phone banking virtual and decentralized in the 2006 elections, and built on this system in 2008. A Yale University study found their system to be the "most effective calling program ever studied." MoveOn volunteers placed over seven million calls during the 2006 election campaign period. As the organization's postelection report explained:

"The core idea is fairly simple—a web-based 'liquid phone bank' allowing MoveOn members to pour calls from wherever they live into wherever they are needed. We could then turn to any district in the country that needed extra attention, and keep the calls flowing until we reached our entire target voters ... Individuals could call from home, using a cutting-edge online tool that walks the user through the script and records the results one call at a time. We also launched a weekly series of phone parties, where members gathered together to make calls on their cell phones."[80]

In the words of Noah Winer, "Elections are a means to an end." All of the election activities MoveOn coordinates are designed to "put pressure on people in office" to keep them responsive to their constituents and aware of what issues those constituents are prioritizing. MoveOn also works to "affect the landscape on which the election fight is happening." Activities like running issue ads, funded by member donations, are key to this effort. [81]

MoveOn has been very successful. Their "Caught Red-Handed" ad campaign in 2006 focused on Chris Chocola (R-IN), Thelma Drake (R-VA), Nancy Johnson (R-CT), and Deborah Pryce (R-OH). Subsequent poll data indicated that after MoveOn's ads, each of these incumbents' negative ratings increased by 5 to 10 percentage points.[82] The "Caught Red-Handed" message was deployed in ads to influence the health care reform debate of 2009 as well.

In order to maximize an organization's impact, it is important to target limited time and resources toward specific races. A MoveOn staffer says, "Two key ingredients for our involvement are, one, doing what members want and two, that there is a decent chance of success, [that our members can affect] the balance." Races are evaluated for competiveness and potential, but even if the odds of victory are small, it may still be advantageous to get involved in order to "fire a shot across the bow" with the message that unresponsive elected officials "will face stiff resistance from the progressive wing of the Democratic Party."[83]

MoveOn was involved in the 2008 primary race for a House seat in Maryland. Their members aided challenger Donna Edwards in defeating incumbent Al Wynn. Of this victory, Noah Winer (formerly with MoveOn) notes: "Although a single member of Congress will not change the decisions of Congress, it is still a powerful victory because others see the consequences of being unresponsive." For those officials "reading the tea leaves," it "changes their calculus" to see progressives affect the election results.

MoveOn capitalizes on these crucial election dynamics by targeting their campaign messages in sensitive districts to increase its effectiveness. For example, MoveOn heavily targeted—with ads and constituent contacts—the officials they helped get elected when they were attempting to define the "public option" in the health care reform as the most critical provision. MoveOn was successful. Their champions in Congress focused most of their energy on promoting the public option.

During the Family and Medical Leave Act campaign in 1992, Democrats controlled both the House and Senate and were able to pass the legislation. President George H.W. Bush, a Republican, vetoed it. The advocates believed that having a Democrat as president would help eliminate the possibility of a veto of the legislation. Therefore, the coalition worked to elect Bill Clinton president by holding events in select media markets to showcase the importance of the issue to mothers and children. Their efforts paid off. President Clinton's first act as president was to sign the Family and Medical Leave Act into law.

But, even well-funded and politically powerful organizations don't get everything they want. The labor movement invested tens of millions of dollars between 1996 and 2010 to promote mostly Democratic candidates. Because of these expenditures and their active efforts to educate their members through "scorecards" that rate the votes of members of Congress, organized labor has enormous access and power. Nonetheless, they had trouble during those years passing legislation barring replacement of union members who are on strike, reforming the National Labor Relations Act, and making union organizing easier. On the other hand, labor helped enact increases in the minimum wage, effectively stalled free-trade legislation, and helped persuade the Obama administration to bail out the auto industry during the great recession of 2009.

Similarly, the NRA in 2009 effectively blocked the DC VRA and got a law passed that allows people to carry concealed weapons in national parks. They could not, however, get a law passed allowing people from "concealed-carry" states to carry firearms around the country. They also could not they defeat the confirmation of Justices Sonia Sotomayor and Elena Kagan, who support a narrow-reading of the second amendment right to "bear arms," because some pro-gun legislators were willing to go against the NRA on those votes.

The Leadership Conference on Civil and Human Rights does not get involved at all in elections. Yet, in 2009 they helped to enact bills, including ones that expand the definition of "hate crimes" and overturn the Supreme Court's decision on a sex discrimination case. They also helped to confirm Justices Sotomayor and Kagan. As Wade Henderson put it, "using your money and your members to affect elections does not necessarily determine your success on the issues." That said a number of their coalition partners (with organized labor being the most prominent) have PACs and are heavily involved in elections.

While getting involved in elections will not guarantee your ability to succeed legislatively, it will certainly give you more power.

The Tools: A Menu of Options

As described in the first eight chapters of this book, human system dynamics offers a wide range of tools for use should your organization decide that you want to promote or defeat a candidate for office.

You can try to create a "butterfly effect" by contributing money to candidates, advertising, holding rallies, hosting house parties, sending e-mails, creating websites, releasing score cards, and sending letters to voters. Each of these activities represents a potential butterfly effect— a small action that might make a major difference in the campaign. Of course, spend time and money if possible researching potential messages before the campaign starts.

Remember, however, that President Obama's campaign manager said that talking to people directly is the most important thing you can do. So, invest in a strong ground operation. Get your people out knocking on doors and urging others to vote for or against your target.

The Bottom Line

1. Elections can make or break your cause.

2. Where possible, work to support the reelection of your supporters and the defeat of your opponents.

3. Your campaign contributions, ads, and/or get-out-the-vote efforts may be the key to winning, so do as much as you can!

4. Above all, create a transforming feedback loop by talking to people directly and convincing them to adopt your position.

X. You Lose Until You Win

Most Successful advocacy campaigns suffer many small and some large defeats along the way to victory, so keep fighting!

The Story

Christmas was just days away. It was the end of 2006. The Republican-led Congress was still in town, moving through a lame-duck session. They just lost their majorities in both the House and the Senate. Congress was working on bills to fund the federal government. Chairman Jim Sensenbrenner (R-WI) held a hearing and a mark-up of the DC Voting Rights Act in September, finally giving us the conservative support we needed. The Utah state legislature took action to help pass the bill. They held a series of town hall hearings during the last week of November before deciding on a four-seat legislative map to accommodate the additional seat they'd get under the DC VRA.[84] The Utah legislature met in an emergency session on December 4, 2006 to enact that map.[85] Utah Governor John Huntsman signed it into law.

Senators Hatch, Bennett, and Lieberman put out a statement saying they would ask the Senate to take up the bill and pass it post-haste. Tom Davis and Jack Kemp asked the House Republican leadership to bring the "Davis Bill" (as the "DC Voting Rights Act" was known then) up for a vote as a way to lock in a Republican success on civil rights.

Representatives John Boehner, Roy Blunt, Eric Cantor, and a couple of others met and decided not to bring the bill up. As reported by the *Washington Post*, "Shameful, sad and worse is the way. . . Jack Kemp, a longtime advocate of D.C. voting rights, characterized the bill's death at the hands of his party."[86] Kemp also said to me, "Republicans never lose an opportunity to screw up a civil rights vote."

A year later, DC Vote suffered another defeat. It was 2007. The Democrats had taken control of the House and Senate. After two committees held hearings and markups and implemented a novel rule change to avoid a gun rights amendment to the bill, the House passed the DC Voting Rights Act in April. We then accelerated our efforts in the Senate. Through our lobbyists and other insiders, we zeroed in on a few key targets: Senators Max Baucus (D-MT), Robert Byrd (D-WV), Thad Cochran (R-MS), Richard Lugar (R-IN), John McCain (R-AZ), Gordon Smith (R-OR), Arlen Specter (at the time, R-PA), and John Warner (R-VA). Baucus and Byrd, we understood, we might lose. Baucus did not like that Utah was getting a seat because he thought Montana should get one. Byrd thought our bill was unconstitutional. The other senators were Republicans whose votes we believed we had a chance to win. In fact, Cochran, McCain, and Smith all told donors and other DC Vote allies who contacted them that they would not support a filibuster.

The Senate vote was on September 18, 2007. A week before the vote on our bill, we learned that the Republican leadership was going all out to defeat us. Mitch McConnell stood up during a Republican caucus meeting and argued aggressively against the bill because he thought it was a slippery slope to two DC Democratic senators and the transformation of DC into a state. Hatch came to our defense by arguing that the bill only impacted the House, but it was too late. By the time the vote occurred, we lost the battle to prevent a filibuster by a vote of fifty-seven to forty-two (sixty absolute votes are needed to end debate, also known as "cloture," in the Senate). Among our opponents were Baucus, Cochran, McCain, and Smith—four senators who decided to oppose us at the last minute.

In truth, these defeats followed many smaller setbacks over a six-year period. After each defeat, pundits and some of our donors assumed that the bill was dead. But, we regrouped each time, adjusted our strategy to take into account different political dynamics, and moved the bill the next time we had an opening in Congress. As of 2012, we were still fighting the good fight for DC democracy.

Additional Stories

The Campaign Finance Reform Act campaign is an example of how success often doesn't occur during the first or second election cycle from the date of introduction. Until 2002, when the campaign gained Republican support, it seemed that the effort was characterized by setback and failure for many years. Groups must be persistent from year-to-year and must not let their energy dissipate. Fighting the fight is only half the battle—the goal is to change public policy! Remember also that once you win, you have to be vigilant because the battle continues. In 2010, opponents of campaign finance reform scored a major victory when the Supreme Court decided in *Citizens United* that corporations have the rights of individuals to spend unlimited resources influencing an election.

Take heart. Many seemingly impossible battles have been waged and won after a marathon effort. The "Free South Africa" campaign showed that dreams certainly can become reality, especially when you engage in an effective civil disobedience campaign where you have moral authority on your side. The campaign in the United States to pressure South Africa to end its apartheid practices began in 1981 and continued through the late eighties, a period during which Republicans controlled the US Senate and the White House. In 1982, US financial involvement in South Africa totaled greater than $14 billion (excluding trade); direct investment by hundreds of corporations at $2.8 billion; outstanding loans by US financial institutions of $3.6 billion; and US-based investors held $8 billion worth of shares in South African mines.

In 1983, there seemed to be no chance of winning. There was no popular surge for legislation in the Congress and the goal of divestment was simply a dream. Then, on the day before Thanksgiving in 1983, four individuals staged a sit-in and refused to leave the South African Embassy in Washington, DC. Their civil disobedience was covered by the media in television broadcasts and on the front pages of newspapers. Civil disobedience at the South African Embassy became an "earned" media event and helped to build a coalition and embolden champions on Capitol Hill. For over a year, there were ritualized arrests at the embassy where "champions" of all forms came day after day to protest apartheid. The issue became popular and chic, both nationally and internationally. Celebrities like Stevie Wonder and other national figures, as well as students, were arrested. The campaign also created a broad coalition of universities and colleges, churches, and other faith-based institutions, labor unions, municipalities, and American states that first started selling off their holdings in South Africa. The "earned" media and the constant pressure on Congress by a public that got involved once the issue was popularized eventually prompted Congress to pass legislation that led to the fall of apartheid in South Africa.

Meredith McGehee of the Campaign Legal Center says legislative fights are "like a marathon race" and take real commitment. Unlike an all-out sprint that requires great effort but ends quickly, in a legislative campaign she warns that you have to keep going steadily to stay in the race and stay positioned for "an opportune moment for the burst of speed where all the things you have been doing come together." She cautions that such an opportunity will likely occur because of something over which you have no control. But you must have been running all along to be in position to take advantage of the opportunity when it does happen. And even then, she says, it is rare that you get 100 percent of what you have been working for, but "that's just part of it," and advocates must be prepared to accept compromise legislation.

Here's an additional example involving the Healthcare Information and Management Systems Society (HIMSS), which helped secure "as much as $36.5 billion in spending" in the 2009 stimulus bill to pursue information technology upgrades and integration in the medical field. HIMSS has a government affairs office in Washington, DC as well as offices in state capitals nationwide, and prides itself on a "very effective grassroots advocacy program that reaches all levels of government." [87] Prior to being awarded 2009 stimulus funding that was designed to get the economy going again, their only high-profile success in many years had been a single line in President Bush's 2004 State of the Union speech favoring computerized medical records. HIMSS patiently and consistently pursued meetings with influential industry and government leaders to push their cause. They, and other allied groups, produced and distributed research advocating investment in information-technology reform and touting huge potential savings from computerizing medical records. Finally, the combination of Obama's election and the economic downturn provided the policy window for HIMSS to present the same solution they had been advocating for years, and to win billions of dollars for their initiative.

The decades-old controversy around the regulation of tobacco products in the US provides yet another example of a win after many years of losses. A strong tobacco industry lobby had prevented strict regulation for decades, successfully holding off proposed legislation, round-after-round. Meanwhile, after a series of successful lawsuits and a growing body of research around tobacco's effects, public opinion about cancer changed, reinforcing the efforts of antitobacco advocates. Control of Congress, and then of the White House, also changed hands from Republicans to Democrats in 2006 and 2008, respectively. After over fifty years of work, legislation giving the federal government new authority to regulate the tobacco industry and curtail its marketing passed easily through Congress and become law in June 2009, with very little fanfare or public attention. [88]

This illustrates an observation by OMB Watch founder Gary Bass. "Advocacy is about persistence," he says. "No fight is ever over, no victory is ever complete." Issues evolve and resurface over time, in new political conditions with new advocates and adversaries. Thus, Bass says, you and your allies must always stay focused on your long term goals, whether it is creating a new legislative opportunity or defending against a new threat to a law you helped get enacted years ago. Keep your eyes on the prize. Be adaptive and ready to change strategy, tactics, and even your message based on changes that emerge. "In my experience," he says, "groups that become less effective tend to take a cookie cutter approach." All issues and instances need a fresh analysis, even if the same coalition is involved.

Terry Lierman, chief of staff to Representative Steny Hoyer, believes that advocates should "keep in mind that you do not have to settle for a one-shot deal. Fight for your cause year-after-year. It is not true that you only get one shot" with a legislature. "Advocacy groups have an obligation to push the ball forward even after you win a legislative victory."

The Tools: Deal with "Sticky Issues" by Using Adaptive Action

Royce Holladay and Kristine Quade put it best when they define a "sticky issue" as "systemic challenges [that] never seem to go away, no matter how many times they are addressed."[89] Sticky issues surface over and over again despite various changes in tactics. These are different from recurring, perennial fights such as those over the budget and taxes, for example. The sticky issues of 2011 included climate change, immigration reform, energy policy, and national education policy. I suppose it can be said that, in the national legislative context, sticky issues are those for which there is not yet broad agreement about the solution as described in the Landscape Diagram in the Introduction.

DC voting rights is a prime example of a sticky issue. We started off with a bill that was a major compromise for the movement; it called for a vote in the

House only, rather than a DC statehood bill, which would create a new state and provide representation in the Senate. That effort was in direct response to the constant failure of more comprehensive efforts to achieve voting representation since the 1970s. Over several years, we changed the bill whenever we hit a roadblock. We made the additional seat in Utah at-large because Judiciary Chairman Jim Sensenbrenner refused to support us without that change. We also permanently expanded the size of the House to 437 members because some legislators voiced opposition to a bill that would effectively reduce the number of seats over which the rest of the country would compete. We added expedited judicial review in the Senate to get the support of Senator Susan Collins. In the House, we split the bill in half and dropped language that would eliminate the Delegate position because of an effort to add a gun amendment to the bill.

Through all these changes and compromises, it has been clear that there are dynamics at work within the Congress that make greater democracy for DC a "sticky issue." Simply put: DC does not have power in the Congress, and therefore we find it very difficult to exert enough pressure on members of Congress—none of whom are indebted to DC voters— to push a bill through, or even to completely resist legislative interference in the District's home rule authority. Also, there isn't enough knowledge in the country about DC's plight, making it hard to get broad agreement on a solution.

The fight for DC democracy continues, nonetheless, because people who live in the District will not rest until they are treated like full American citizens with equal rights to representation and local control. In this sense, DC democracy is a sticky issue because this injustice cannot stand. So, the fight continues, as does DC's lack of power to get Congress to take action.

When faced with a sticky issue, advocates must respond by being flexible and adaptive to new circumstances. It is also very important to look at the places where problems emerge and to deal with those challenges directly. Use the Adaptive Action Model (Chapter III, Diagram 3) to figure out: what do you see, what it means, and what do you do now.

The answers to these questions may illustrate the need for more fundamental change, such as altering your message, the legislation you are pursuing, or even your mission. Making any one of these changes is a high-risk effort because you will, in essence, alter your "container" (i.e., the things by which people identify your organization). You may lose some donors or coalition allies by making these changes, while potentially recruiting new people to your effort.

In 2009 and 2010, DC Vote decided to expand our mission to include a fight for local democracy and to embrace a much more aggressive protest strategy. We had the votes in the 111th Congress to pass the DC Voting Rights Act and President Barack Obama was ready to sign it into law. But pro-gun forces in Congress, led by Democratic Majority Leader Harry Reid, supported an amendment to the DC VRA that would have eliminated DC's gun control laws and its home rule authority to enact such laws in the future. This "poison pill" amendment was repulsive to DC residents and elected officials and made passage of the DC VRA impossible.[90]

In the face of this defeat of a compromise bill that benefitted Republicans more than Democrats (Republicans received an entirely new seat and an additional Electoral College vote for Utah), we decided to focus much more on an aggressive outside game strategy of escalating protests, including civil disobedience, by DC residents and the government.

This "Demand Democracy Campaign" was a major shift for DC Vote. We reembraced the outside game strategy we pursued in 2000 because we no longer had viable legislative vehicles for our champions to move through Congress. In the Landscape Diagram (see Introduction), we agreed on the merits of the DC Voting Rights Act. But, we lost certainty over whether it would pass because of the gun amendment to that bill. Like other campaigns, this one will highly depend on us maintaining the moral high ground and getting Americans to call their representatives and senators in support of democracy and equality for DC residents. Ultimately, this aggressive outside game, we believe, is necessary to create the political space for us to return to the inside game once again, where we will directly engage members of the House and Senate in moving legislation.

The Bottom Line

1. Advocacy fights are marathons, not sprints.

2. Legislative victories are won through movements that combine outside and inside game strategies, and movements must be sustained over a period of time with regular activities designed to keep stakeholders engaged and enthusiastic about the goal.

3. Be persistent and determined to achieve success over the long haul.

4. Be adaptive and ready to make major shifts in your strategies, goals, tactics, and mission to overcome consistent opposition.

Conclusion

Legislative action in 2009 on the DC Voting Rights Act (VRA) represents a great example of how adhering to the strategies in this book helps move your issue forward. Senator Harry Reid put the DC VRA before the Senate for a full vote on February 26, 2009 for the below reasons.

Frame the Issue and Avoid Extremes

We sought bipartisanship right away by framing our issue as a voting rights issue. In light of past failed attempts to achieve comprehensive reform, we focused on voting representation in Congress, rather than statehood. Reid supports DC statehood, but Senators Collins, Hatch, Voinovich, Snowe, and other senators whose votes we needed, have told us publicly and privately that they would oppose statehood. Therefore, we would not have had the votes for the bill. Reid would certainly not have put a statehood bill before the Senate for a vote.

Recruit the Right Champions

We also cultivated a strong working relationship with two very important champions in the Senate, Joe Lieberman and Orrin Hatch (Representative Tom Davis had retired from the Congress in 2008). Lieberman was chair of the Homeland Security and Governmental Affairs Committee (the committee that has jurisdiction over DC issues). Thus he could and did schedule an early markup of the bill. Hatch, a Republican from Utah (a state which stood to benefit from the bill), made it easier for other Republicans to support our bill. As a former chairman of the Judiciary Committee and with a reputation as a legislative expert on the constitutional questions, Hatch's argument that the DC VRA was constitutional greatly helped legitimize our assertions. Also, Eleanor Holmes Norton was a tenacious "street fighter," constantly demanding that legislative leaders take action. Most House and Senate Democratic leaders find it very difficult to ignore her demands.

Lead a Working Coalition and Give People a Chance to Fight

Our coalition partners and individual supporters helped us get constituents in targeted states to contact their Senators, thereby increasing the vote count in favor of the DC VRA. Also, Senators Reid and Lieberman care a lot about civil rights organizations. Both Senators like being heroes of the civil rights movement because that helps them demonstrate a commitment to civil rights constituencies (minorities, liberal Democrats, and civil-rights-minded independents) in their states and/or in Congress.

Direct the Outside Game to Decision-Makers

Additionally, our activities on and off the Hill helped generate over 3,000 news stories, which helped build support in Congress. *The New York Times* and the *Washington Post* (as well as many regional papers) editorialized numerous times in support of the DC VRA. People like Senator Reid, and even Senator Hatch, want to be applauded by the national media. Therefore, by moving a bill that has support in the media and draws national attention, legislative leaders increase their profile, which in turn helps them raise money and win elections.

Elections Matter

The gun amendment offered by Senator John Ensign (R-NV) changed the dynamics and patterns around our bill.[91] For Reid, his reelection trumped everything else. He decided he could not afford to get an F-score from the NRA because that would make him much more vulnerable in Nevada, where he was facing a strong challenger for his seat in 2010. So, he voted for the gun amendment, protecting himself from the NRA. He also got to vote for the DC VRA, giving him a civil rights vote. In politics, as elsewhere, that is called a "twofer."

Twenty-two pro-gun Democrats, believing they received a green light from Reid, voted for a gun amendment to ingratiate themselves with the NRA. They understood that elections matter.

You Lose Until You Win

Of course, that is not the end of the story. we understood Principle X: you lose until you win. We kept fighting and adjusting our strategy. Ultimately, DC Vote decided that we needed to unify the movement and our elected officials by expanding our mission to include a fight for local democracy and explicitly stating our support for eventually turning DC into the fifty-first state of New Columbia. We also began working with DC City Council and other officials to create our Demand Democracy Campaign. We switched back to the outside game in order to gain much more national attention, increase the active support of the American people, and force Congress to take positive action on our issue in order to stop us.

DC Vote's goal was to shift our container away from a focus on the DC VRA back to the problem of taxation without representation. We would make the exchanges much more vigorous through aggressive protest actions. DC Vote's hope was that these containers and exchanges would place a spotlight on the key difference between DC and our legislative opponents: DC residents want full equality and democracy and our opponents want to keep treating DC like it is a modern day colony. If the American people focus on the differences from that vantage point, then we have a chance of winning and making the fight for DC democracy something that is no longer a sticky issue, but just another chapter in our nation's history.

APPENDIX: The Ten Strategies

I. Frame Your Issue First

Your message and legislative strategy are deeply intertwined and must be developed through research.

The Bottom Line

1. First, frame your request for legislative change in a way that maximizes legislative and public support.

2. Conduct polls and focus groups, if possible, when developing your message.

3. Apply the "Container, Differences, and Exchanges" concept to figure out the best way to frame your issue.

4. Gauge the reaction of legislators and their staff before you decide what you ask for and how you talk about it.

II. Recruit the Right Champions

Your champions will be essential during the legislative process, so choose wisely and build a relationship of trust.

The Bottom Line

1. All legislative efforts are dependent on legislative champions taking up your cause and doing the hard work to get the bill passed.

2. Find the right champion by figuring out which legislative committee has jurisdiction over your issue.

3. Try to interest the person who is both passionate about your issue and has power (e.g., the person who has seniority and perhaps is chair or ranking legislator).

4. When you find your champion(s), remember that the staff plays a pivotal role in how effective you will be; therefore, cultivate a relationship of trust with the champion's staff and stay in frequent contact.

5. Your champion will help you understand the patterns at work, and use those patterns to your advantage.

III. Secure Votes by Avoiding Extremes

Get a jump on the legislative process by starting with the bill that you believe will engender broad support and is most likely to pass

The Bottom Line

1. Understand that your bill will create patterns of behavior in Congress that will be hard to change later.

2. Where possible, begin the legislative process by recruiting bipartisan and/or broad support at the outset before your bill is created.

3. To secure enough votes, develop a bill that will attract a range of legislative champions and thus significantly increase your chances of success.

4. Use the Adaptive Action Model to at each stage of the bill development.

IV. Lead a Working Coalition

Create or Join a coalition of organizations with a common interest and enable them to magnify your collective power.

The Bottom Line

1. Broad national coalitions are needed to popularize the issue, to capture the attention of the media and to attract champions. Just as important, they are necessary to do advocacy legwork.

2. National coalitions help you target specific districts in the states by asking people to contact their legislators.

3. Expect different levels of commitment and engagement from different coalition members based on their capacity and commitment to the coalition's mission.

4. Coalitions require on-going efforts and hard work to keep the movement alive even when there is no legislative action.

5. Use the HSD models to decide your appropriate container and the degree of differences you want to encourage within your coalition.

V. Empower the Grassroots

When people fight for their rights, they create energy that is critical to your mission.

The Bottom Line

1. The people who are most directly affected by the problem you are trying to solve are among your strongest advocates. Give them a voice.

2. Look for and incorporate the voices of people who may not be your most obvious allies or supporters.

3. Engage the grassroots by enabling people to contact legislators or attend a rally.

4. Give people the opportunity to be creative in their advocacy—they may surprise you and give your movement some real momentum.

5. Be ready to engage in direct action and even civil disobedience to ensure your voice is heard.

VI. Use the Outside Game to Influence Policymakers

Find ways to ensure that you link your activities to the ultimate goal: Achieving Social Change.

The Bottom Line

1. Winning the inside game starts with recruiting outside supporters.

2. Engage in activity outside the halls of the legislative and executive branch that generates news stories because they impact perceptions among the inside players.

3. Create a cycle where "outside game" activities result in media stories, which result in more legislative attention, which feeds your recruitment of people for grassroots activities.

4. Ultimately, most of your activities should aim to increase your presence and influence among decision makers.

VII. Communicate at All Times in All Directions

Use websites, e-mail, social networks, and newsletters to communicate with everyone, but don't forget that talking to people directly is still most effective

The Bottom Line

1. Organizations have to communicate in all directions at all times.

2. You cannot assume that your message is getting through to the right people or that they understand it.

3. The most effective way to communicate with people is by talking to them directly.

4. Utilize all the modern tools of communication; make sure you create and maintain a comprehensive website.

5. Refuse to make assumptions about boundaries between you and others.

6. Where possible, cross boundaries often.

VIII. Work the Inside Game

Advocacy organizations must use their Board members, donors, lobbyists, and others to directly engage legislators and their staff.

The Bottom Line

1. Place a premium on direct interaction with legislators and their staff.

2. Ensure you can provide quality information on a moment's notice.

3. Be honest and straightforward with your legislative allies.

4. Build credibility by resisting the temptation to exaggerate or stretch the facts.

5. Create and participate in face-to-face transforming feedback loops.

6. Follow up!

IX. Elections Matter

You can become a more effective advocate if your organization works to promote and defeat candidates.

The Bottom Line

1. Elections can make or break your cause.

2. Where possible, work to support the reelection of your supporters and the defeat of your opponents.

3. Your campaign contributions, ads, and/or get-out-the-vote efforts may be the key to winning, so do as much as you can!

4. Above all, create a transforming feedback loop by talking to people directly and convincing them to adopt your position.

X. You Lose Until You Win

Most Successful advocacy campaigns suffer many small and some large defeats along the way to victory, so keep fighting!

The Bottom Line

1. Advocacy fights are marathons, not sprints.

2. Legislative victories are won through movements that combine outside and inside game strategies, and movements must be sustained over a period time with regular activities designed to keep stakeholders engaged and enthusiastic about the goal.

3. Be persistent and determined to achieve success over the long haul.

4. Be adaptive and ready to make major shifts in your strategies, goals, tactics, and mission to overcome consistent opposition.

ENDNOTES

1. The Trover Shop, founded in 1958 and located blocks from the Capitol, was a local landmark and political watering hole for Hill staffers. The family-owned store had hosted book-signings for every Speaker since Tip O'Neill, along with many other prominent political authors. In July 2009, the bookstore announced plans to close, citing the economy and online competitors. See White, Jeremy B. 2009. Trover Shop to Close after 51 Years on Hill. *Roll Call.* July 9, 22. http://www.rollcall.com/issues/55_3/ath/36545-1.html (accessed July 9, 2009).
2. For more, see the HSD website. Human Systems Dynamics Institute. "About HSD." http://www.hsdinstitute.org/about-hsd/what-is-hsd.html (accessed September 8, 2009).
3. See Article I, Section 8, clause 17 of the US Constitution.
4. A local resident, Augustus Woodward, wrote three columns, written under the pen-name "Epaminondas," arguing against stripping District residents of their political rights at the end of 1800. Each column appeared under a header title "Considerations on the Government of the Territory of Columbia."
   No. 1: *National Intelligencer* (DC), December 24, 1800, 1. Also reprinted in *Alexandria Times and District of Columbia Daily Advertiser* (VA), December 27, 1800, 2-3; No. 2: *National Intelligencer,* December 26, 1800, 3; No. 3: *National Intelligencer,* December 29, 1800, 4. No. 4: *National Intelligencer,* December 31, 1800.
   These articles are accessible online at:
   http://www.dcvote.org/trellis/struggle/woodward_epaminondas_national_intelligencer_1800.pdf
   See also: Green, Constance McLaughlin. 1962. *Washington: Village and Capital, 1800-1878.* Princeton, NJ: Princeton University Press, 24-25.

5. Although people usually use the term "legislator" to refer to legislators of the House of Representatives and "senator" is the term used for legislators of the Senate, I use "Legislators" throughout this book to refer to both.

6. Holladay, Royce and Kristine Quade, 2008. Influencing Patterns for Change: A Human Dynamics Primer for Leaders. Self-published manuscript, 61.

7. Holladay & Quade, 29-33. The Landscape Diagram illustrates the flow of people, work, and information involved in organizational work. It shows "the lay of the land" and the patterns formed as people move from uncertainty to agreement.

8. Singer, Paul. 2008. Legislators Offered Many Bills but Passed Few. *Roll Call*, December 1, 2008. Washington, DC: CQ-Roll Call Inc.

9. United States House of Representatives. Office of the Clerk. "Final Vote Results for Roll Call 595." http://clerk.house.gov/evs/1993/roll595.xml

10. Among the Democrats were Steny Hoyer (D-MD) and Jim Moran (D-VA).

11. In 1987, barely more than half of survey respondents nationwide supported DC Statehood. "Asked whether they agreed or disagreed with a bill to grant statehood to the District, 52 percent agreed, nearly 24 percent disagreed and 24 percent had no opinion."
Pianin, Eric. Poll on D.C. Rights 'Yes, but...' Empathy For Representation Doesn't Extend to Statehood. *Washington Post*. May 16. B3
Eight years later, and a year and a half after the statehood vote in Congress, a Washington Post poll showed that even within the District, support for Statehood had dropped below 50%. Yolanda Woodlee and Richard Morin. 1995. D.C. Residents See a Future at Risk; Blacks, Whites Split Over Plans to Appoint Control Board, Poll Shows. *Washington Post*. March 5, 1995. A1
By 2006, statehood polled even worse nationally. Of 1,011 randomly selected adults, 22 percent were in favor and 20 percent were undecided. Montgomery, Lori. March 24, 2006. Blog post. DC Wire. http://blog.washingtonpost.com/dcwire/2006/03/dc_statehood_popular_as_dirt.html (accessed June 25, 2009).

12. Visit the DC Vote website to review a poll demonstrating the overwhelming support of Americans for full equality and democracy for DC residents: http://www.dcvote.org/trellis/section.cfm?trellisID=25.

13. Richards, Mark David. 2005. US Public Opinion on DC Voting Rights. Survey conducted for DC Vote. Report available online at: http://www.dcvote.org/pdfs/polls/polljan2005.pdf

14. April 19, 2007 LEGISLATIVE RECORD—HOUSE H3585-H3586. http://frwebgate.access.gpo.gov/cgi-bin/getpage.cgi?position=all&page= H3586&dbname=2007_record (accessed May 12, 2009).

15. MoveOn, an organization that caught fire in 1998 with both grassroots and netroots organizing, and has as its mission "to bring real Americans back into the political process." Noah T. Winer, who has served for six years on the staff of MoveOn, emphasizes that everything the organization does depends on research. MoveOn relies on its own internal polling as well as public opinion research done by others. To underscore the importance of using research, Winer cited the ongoing campaign for health care reform. Even though MoveOn was not positioned to conduct its own research, MoveOn used polling data showing that the ideas of competition among healthcare providers and lower pricing were strong messages that resonated with the public. They used two studies estimating the cost savings that would be possible if public health insurance options were offered. Then they translated that information into a call to action, urging their legislators in an e-mail to fax a "30% off healthcare with Obama's public insurance option" coupon to key Legislators of Congress. This allowed the campaign to more forcefully convey what the research had showed was at stake for Americans' healthcare options. By using these external sources of research, MoveOn was able to create a more compelling campaign for healthcare reform and elevate the importance of publicly financed healthcare options, a key priority for its legislators.

16. Craig, Tim. 2009. Friends, Foes of Same-Sex Marriage Monitor District's Legislative Moves. *Washington Post*, May 5, Metro B Section.

17. McKibben, Bill. 2010. Record snows on a warming planet. *Washington Post*. February 14, B1.

18. Did D.C.'s blizzard bury climate change legislation? *Washington Post*. February 14, 2010. http://www.washingtonpost.com/wp-dyn/content/article/2010/02/12/AR2010021203910.html (accessed August 28, 2010) and Milbank, Dana. 2010. "Global warming's snowball fight," *Washington Post*. February 14, A21. http://www.washingtonpost.com/wp-dyn/content/article/2010/02/12/AR2010021203908.html (accessed August 28, 2010).

19. Milbank, Dana. 2010. "Global warming's snowball fight," *Washington Post*. February 14, A21.

20. See the organization's website, http://www.commoncause.org/site/pp.asp?c=dkLNKIMQIwG&b=4860183 (accessed April 22, 2009).

21. Holladay & Quade, 16.

22. Among the many such instructive guides are: *Hardball Lobbying For Nonprofits : Real Advocacy for Nonprofits in the New Century,* **by Barry Hessenius** (2007); Michael Gecan's *Going Public: An Organizer's Guide to Citizen Action* (2004), Rinku Sen's *Stir It Up: Lessons in Community Organizing and Advocacy* (2003); Marcia Avner's *Lobbying and Advocacy Handbook for Nonprofit Organizations: Shaping Public Policy at the State and Local Level* (2002); and Bob Smucker's *The Nonprofit Lobbying Guide* (2nd Edition, 1999). Also, visit the website for the Center for Lobbying in the Public Interest at www.clpi.org.

23. Eoyang, 52.

24. Eoyang, 50.

25. Pierce, Emily. 2009. Schumer Legislates Like He Campaigns. *Roll Call.* October 2, page 1. http://www.rollcall.com/issues/55_50/news/40129-1.html (accessed on August 28, 2010).

26. In order to protect the best interests of the ongoing campaign for DC voting rights, and to enable high-profile contributors to this book to speak frankly, the author is occasionally obliged to protect the anonymity and confidentiality of some sources.

27. The number of bills introduced in each Congress has risen steadily in recent years. In the 104th Congress (1995-1996), 6,542 bills were introduced, increasing to 7,529 in the 105th (1997-1998). The 106th (1999-2000), 107th (2001-2002), and 108th (2003-2004) sessions of Congress each had introductions in the high 8,000s. During the 109th Congress (2005-2006), over 10,000 bills were introduced. Harper, Jim. August 4, 2008. "10,000 Bills Introduced in Congress, While Government Management Goes Neglected." The Hill's Congress Blog, *The Hill* newspaper. http://blog.thehill.com/2008/08/04/10000-bills-introduced-in-congress-while-government-management-goes-neglected/) (accessed June 25, 2009).

28. The Library of Congress. "About Floor Actions." http://www.thomas.gov/home/floor.html

29. You may wish to develop and have introduced a bill which embodies all your aspirations. This strategy would make sense during an education phase of your work when you are trying to inform Legislators and their staff about the changes you are seeking. Such a bill, however, is not something that you

would necessarily try to move through Congress because the chances of your getting bipartisan support would likely be low.

30. That 60-vote threshold was set for countering filibusters in 1975. Since then, there have been only two instances – in the 94th and 95th sessions of Congress, between 1975 and 1979 – when a party has held an overwhelming number of Senate seats and, therefore, the power to impose its will. United States Senate. "Party Division in the Senate, 1789-Present." http://www.senate.gov/pagelayout/history/one_item_and_teasers/partydiv.htm

31. Arlen Specter had not yet switched parties and become a Democrat. Al Franken, a Democrat, had not yet been seated due to vote recounts in Minnesota. Scott Brown, a Republican, would not win the Massachusetts race until January of 2010.

32. Warren, Timothy. 2009. Senate passes key vote on D.C. voting. *The Washington Times*, Feb 24. http://www.washingtontimes.com/news/2009/feb/24/senate-passes-key-vote-dc-voting/ (accessed May 6, 2009).

33. The Republican votes were cast by Senators Cochran (R-MS), Collins (R-ME), Hatch (R-UT), Lugar (R-IN), Murkowski (R-AK), Snowe (R-ME), Specter (R-PA) and Voinovich (R-OH). *See* Senatus. 2009. Senate Votes to Move D.C. Voting Rights Bill Forward. Senatus: Daily Coverage of the United States Senate, Feb 24. http://senatus.wordpress.com/2009/02/24/senate-votes-to-move-dc-voting-rights-bill-forward/ (accessed May 6, 2009).

34. See the organization's website, http://www.csgv.org/site/c.pmL5JnO7KzE/b.3509221/k.C716/About_Us.htm (accessed April 22, 2009).

35. See the organization's website, http://www.civilrights.org/about/ (accessed April 22, 2009).

36. Montgomery, Lori. 2011. Senate Democrats keep budget close to the vest: Say releasing details might stymie Biden's bipartisan talks. The Washington Post. May 20, A4. http://www.washingtonpost.com/business/economy/senate-democrats-wont-release-their-spending-plan/2011/05/19/AFhrIP7G_story.html (accessed January 20, 2012).

37. Halloday & Quade, 45-46.

38. Burr, Thomas. 2006. Breaking: Utah Hoping to Get Fourth Seat in US House. *Salt Lake Tribune* (UT), May 19. http://www.dcvote.org/media/media.cfm?mediaID=1263&year=2006 (accessed May 12, 2009).

39. Sheridan, Mary Beth. 2006. House Panel Endorses D.C. Vote-Davis Secures Passage; Bill Needs Approval From Judiciary Committee. *Washington Post.* May 19, B01. http://www.washingtonpost.com/wp-dyn/content/article/2006/05/18/AR2006051801407.html (accessed May 12, 2009).

40. Montgomery, Lori and Elissa Silverman. 2006. D.C. Vote's Stars Are Aligning, Davis Says. *Washington Post.* May 12, A01.

41. McCormack, Kelly. 2007. "Senate Panel Approves D.C. Voting Bill." *The Hill,* Thursday, Jun 14.

42. Hoover, Nick. 2005. Fulfilling the democratic promise. *DC Examiner.* July 4, 5. http://www.dcvote.org/pdfs//DCExaminerJuly4th05.pdf (accessed May 12, 2009).

43. Yehle, Emily. 2009. Hoyer Wants Fast Action on D.C. Bill. *Roll Call.* Jan 28. http://www.rollcall.com/issues/54_79/news/31810-1.html (accessed July 9, 2009). "Mr. Gohmert said that the city's license plates proclaiming "taxation without representation" had gotten to him." See quote in: Editorial. 2009. D.C. in the House; No representation with no taxation doesn't work, either. Washington Post. February 16, A14. http://www.washingtonpost.com/wp-dyn/content/article/2009/02/15/AR2009021501428.html?hpid=opinionsbox1 (accessed July 9, 2009).

44. Representative Gohmert sponsored the No Taxation Without Representation Act, HR 1014, introduced in the House on February 12, 2009. http://frwebgate.access.gpo.gov/cgi-bin/getdoc.cgi?dbname=111_cong_bills&docid=f:h1014ih.txt.pdf (accessed May 12, 2009).

45. Peters, Jeremy W., 2009. Gay Rights Marchers Press Cause in Washington. *New York Times,* October 11. http://www.nytimes.com/2009/10/12/us/politics/12protest.html?scp=1&sq=gay%20rights%20rally&st=cse (accessed October 15, 2009).

46. Hernandez, Nelson and Yamiche Alcindor, 2009. Making a Federal Case for Gay Rights. *Washington Post,* October 12, A1. http://www.washingtonpost.com/wp-dyn/content/article/2009/10/11/AR2009101100161.html?sub=AR (accessed October 15, 2009).

47. See the organization's website. http://www.moveon.org/about.html (accessed April 22, 2009).

48. Debonis, Mike. 2010. Activists get meeting with key Senate gun-bill sponsor. *Washington Post- DC Wire Blog.* May 20. http://voices.washingtonpost.com/dc/2010/05/activists_get_meeting_with_key.html (accessed September 12, 2010)

McSherry, Alison. 2010. Tester Parries Group's Plea to Abandon Bill on D.C. Gun Laws. *Roll Call*. May 20. Available at: http://www.rollcall.com/news/46464-1.html.

McKee, Jennifer. 2010. D.C. clergy to Tester: Drop your gun bill. *Billings Gazette*. May 20. http://billingsgazette.com/news/state-and-regional/montana/article_9b791106-6461-11df-b210-001cc4c03286.html (accessed September 12, 2010)

King, Ledyard. 2010. Tester says no to D.C. anti-gun activists. *Great Falls Tribune*. May 21. Available at: http://www.dcvote.org/media/media.cfm?mediaID=3180&year=2010 (accessed September 12, 2010)

49. For more information about direct action and civil disobedience activities, see: Ruckus Society: http://www.ruckus.org/ACT UP (Aids Coalition to Unleash Power): http://www.actupny.org/documents/CDdocuments/CDindex.html (Accessed August 28, 2010)

50. Royce Holladay created the voice model.

51. "In general, no organization may qualify for section 501(c)(3) status if a substantial part of its activities is attempting to influence legislation (commonly known as *lobbying*)... Organizations may, however, involve themselves in issues of public policy without the activity being considered as lobbying. For example, organizations may conduct educational meetings, prepare and distribute educational materials, or otherwise consider public policy issues in an educational manner without jeopardizing their tax-exempt status." See Internal Revenue Service. January 6, 2009. Lobbying. http://www.irs.gov/charities/article/0,,id=163392,00.html (accessed April 16, 2009).

52. Fisher, Marc. 2009. Hard Line on Guns Could Set Back D.C. Voting Rights. *Washington Post*. March 12. http://www.washingtonpost.com/wp-dyn/content/article/2009/03/11/AR2009031103574.html (Accessed on August 28, 2010)

53. Jack Kemp was a congressman from New York from 1971 to 1989, served as the Secretary of Housing and Urban Development under President George H. W. Bush, and was the vice presidential nominee on the Republican presidential ticket with Robert Dole in 1996.

54. Kemp, Jack. September 27, 2005. Republican Support for D.C. Citizens. Human Events.com. http://www.dcvote.org/media/media.cfm?mediaID=1131&year=2005 (accessed April 22, 2009).

55. Eoyang, 11.

56. Eoyang, 12.

57. Brower, Michael and Warren Leon. 1999. *The Consumer's Guide to Effective Environmental Choices: Practical Advice from the Union of Concerned Scientists.* Three Rivers Press.

58. Gladwell, Malcolm. 2000. The Tipping Point. Little, Brown, and Company: New York, New York. 38.

59. ibid. 41, 48.

60. Gladwell, 49.

61. Gladwell, 51.

62. Gladwell, 32.

63. DiJulio, Sarah and Andrea Wood. 2009. Online Tactics Success: An Examination of the Obama for America New Media Campaign. M&R Strategic Services, page 2. www.wilburforce.org/pdf/Online_Tactics_and_Success.pdf. *Accessed on August 28, 2010.*

64. Federal Election Commission. 2009. Number of Federal PACs Increases. News Release, March 9. http://www.fec.gov/press/press2009/20090309PACcount.shtml (accessed on August 28, 2010).
Federal Election Commission, 2010. PAC Activity Remains Steady in 2009. News Release, April 6. http://fec.gov/press/press2010/20100406PAC.shtml (accessed on August 28, 2010).

65. Eoyang, 18.

66. Eoyang, 25.

67. Center for Responsive Politics. "Lobbying Database: Overview" at http://www.opensecrets.org/lobby/index.php and "Top Spenders, 2009" at http://www.opensecrets.org/lobby/top.php?showYear=2009&indexType=s

68. Brotherton, Elizabeth. D.C. Voting Rights Bill Passes First Markup, Set for Second. *Roll Call,* March 14. http://www.rollcall.com/issues/52_93/news/17518-1.html (accessed May 6, 2009).

69. Pence, Michael. March 17, 2007. Why I Voted for D.C. Representation in the House. *Human Events.com* http://www.humanevents.com/article.php?id=19858 (accessed April 22, 2009).

70. Sheridan, Mary Beth and Yolanda Woodlee. 2007. House Approves A Full D.C. Seat. *Washington Post.* April 20, A01.

71. Rich, Frank, 2009. The Rabbit Ragu Democrats. *New York Times,* October 3. http://www.nytimes.com/2009/10/04/opinion/04rich.html?_r=1 (accessed October 15, 2009).

72. Eoyang, 29.

73. Eoyang, 35.

74. Wiener, Elizabeth. 2010. Norton: DC Will Get Voting Rights Early This Year. *The Currents (DC)*. January 6. Section: Voice of the Hill.
Editorial. 2010. D.C. voting rights? Not this deal; A poison pill on guns forces a tough decision. *Washington Post*. April 18. A16.

75. See the official National Rifle Association website at http://www.nra.org/aboutus.aspx and the NRA Institute for Legislative Action at http://www.nraila.org/About/

76. Visit the website for the Center for Lobbying in the Public Interest at www.clpi.org for more information about the role of different types of nonprofit organizations and the law governing election-related activities.

77. Zigas, Eli. 2008. Left with Few Rights: Unequal Democracy and the District of Columbia. Self-published manuscript, 35. Accessible at: www.dcvote.org/pdfs/papers/zigas_left_with_few_rights.pdf.

78. Zigas, 43-47.

79. Statistics drawn from: MoveOnPolitical Action. 2008. People-Powered Politics 2008: Post-Election Report.
http://s3.moveon.org/pdfs/moveon_postelectionreport_ah14.pdf (accessed August 25, 2009).

80. MoveOn Political Action. 2006. Election 2006: People Powered Politics - What 3.2 Million Determined MoveOn Legislators Can Do. http://pol.moveon.org/2006report/ (accessed August 25, 2009).

81. Author interview, August 14, 2009.

82. MoveOn Political Action, 2006.

83. Author interview, August 14, 2009.

84. Canham, Matt. 2006. Legislators Want Public to Weigh in on 4 Maps. *Salt Lake Tribune (UT)*, November 25.

85. Emerling, Gary. 2006. Utah Redistricting Brings D.C. Closer to Vote. *Washington Times*, December 5, Metropolitan Section.

86. Editorial. 2006. Shameful, Sad, and Worse. *Washington Post*. December 8. http://www.washingtonpost.com/wp-dyn/content/article/2006/12/07/AR2006120701580.html (accessed April 29, 2009).

87. O'Harrow, Jr., Robert. 2009. The Machinery Behind Healthcare Reform. *Washington Post*. May 16, A1.

88. Fletcher, Michael A. 2009. Obama Signs Bill Regulating Tobacco. *Washington Post*. June 23, A3.

89. Holladay & Quade, 9.

90. Tau, Byron. 2010. How the Gun Lobby Shot Down DC's Legislative Vote. *Washington City Paper*. June 4. http://www.washingtoncitypaper.com/articles/38982/how-the-gun-lobby-shot-down-dcs-legislative-vote-the (accessed on August 28, 2010).

91. See Editorial. 2009. Editorial: What Works for Mr. Ensign . . .; *Washington Post*. June 18, A22. *See also* Nicholas, Stefan C. 2009. Tell Sen. Ensign: The District is Not Nevada. *Washington Business Journal*. June 19. http://washington.bizjournals.com/washington/stories/2009/06/22/editorial3.html?surround=etf&b=1245643200^1847477 (accessed July 9, 2009).